Emma Isaacs is the founder of Business Chicks, a half-million strong community of businesswomen. A born entrepreneur, Emma has spent her life building businesses and helping people see possibility when they hadn't imagined it before.

When Emma was just eighteen, she became the co-owner of a small recruitment company where she had just started working. By the time she sold the business eight years later, it had grown exponentially and was named Australia's Favorite Recruiter in the SEEK Awards for three years in a row.

When Emma was twenty-five, and while she was still running the recruitment company, she felt pulled to try something new. She was invited to a small event by a group called Business Chicks, where she learned the brand was up for sale. She took a leap of faith and bought it.

Over the past sixteen years, Emma has transformed Business Chicks from the ground up, growing it from 250 members to what it is today: a global enterprise that operates in two continents and eleven cities, and produces more than 100 events annually, with past speakers including Dr. Brené Brown, Seth Godin, Sir Richard Branson, Gloria Steinem, Nicole Kidman, Sir Bob Geldof, Sarah Jessica Parker and Julia Gillard, among others.

Born and raised in Sydney, Emma lives in Los Angeles with her six young children, where she heads up the now international Business Chicks. She is a serial property investor, mentor and angel investor, and under her leadership, Business Chicks has raised more than $9 million for charity.

Also by Emma Isaacs

Winging It

EMMA ISAACS

THE NEW HUSTLE

DON'T WORK HARDER, JUST WORK BETTER

NEW YORK CHICAGO SAN FRANCISCO ATHENS LONDON
MADRID MEXICO CITY MILAN NEW DELHI
SINGAPORE SYDNEY TORONTO

1 2 3 4 5 6 7 8 9   LCR   27 26 25 24 23 22

ISBN   978-1-264-90056-5
MHID   1-264-90056-2

e-ISBN   978-1-264-90575-1
e-MHID   1-264-90575-0

First published 2021 in Macmillan by Pan Macmillan Australia Pty Ltd
1 Market Street, Sydney, New South Wales, Australia, 2000

Library of Congress Cataloging-in-Publication Data
Names: Isaacs, Emma, author.
Title: The new hustle : don't work harder, just work better / Emma Isaacs.
Description: Sydney, New South Wales : Macmillan, 2021. | Includes
   bibliographical references and index.
Identifiers: LCCN 2022020015 (print) | LCCN 2022020016 (ebook) |
   ISBN 9781264900565 (hardback) | ISBN 9781264905751 (ebook)
Subjects: LCSH: Psychology, Industrial. | Success. | Burn out (Psychology) |
   Time management.
Classification: LCC HF5548.8 .I729 2021 (print) | LCC HF5548.8 (ebook) |
   DDC 158.7—dc23/eng/20220511
LC record available at https://lccn.loc.gov/2022020015
LC ebook record available at https://lccn.loc.gov/2022020016

To the past, present and future team members of
Business Chicks, who create magic every day

Contents

the old way
of working
is dead.

Often it takes a crisis for us to wake up.

Unknown

This book is a happy accident. It was never intended for public consumption.

You see, at the same time my publishers were gently nudging me and asking, "What is book number two going to be about?," the team at Business Chicks tasked me with a couple of jobs. The first job was to sharpen up our values and vision, and the second was to reshape our company playbook: a resource our team members—old or new—could pick up at any time to get more from their work and understand "the way things are done around here."

You might think it's strange that a founder is given these projects. Don't we have marketing teams and writers and public relations execs and communications experts who can do this for us? We do. We have plenty of them. And they're really smart, talented people too.

But for me, rewriting the company playbook was *the* most important job I could undertake at the time. Over the years, I've learned that a lot of companies make a mistake when they try to outsource this kind of work to someone else. They think the founder or CEO's time should be reserved for strategy and finance, when in reality the biggest gains for a business can often be found in getting back to the original reason a business was started. That reason needs to be extracted from the founder's head so that everyone understands what's important to the founder, whose rules—written or unspoken—become ingrained in everything they do.

The two tasks that the team gave me quickly became a happy distraction. While avoiding emails from my publisher, I got into flow and could write about our way of working for hours on end without looking up or needing a glass of water. The renewed focus on vision and values became like a North Star— lighting the way and guiding us forward—and the company playbook . . . well, this became a treasure trove.

Revisiting the pages of our own playbook brought me back to why, as a young and hopeful entrepreneur, I'd started businesses in the first place. It re-engaged me to our purpose and got me excited again about our future together. It was a reminder of what I wanted for the business I'd built, but also what I wanted from and for the people who brought my vision to life every day.

You see, for a while there I really felt we'd lost our way. We were just getting too comfortable. Complacent even. We were doing things the way they had always been done, instead of interrogating the way we worked and questioning if it was really serving us. There were too many meetings creeping into everyone's calendars, and I was listening to my team complaining that they didn't have time to do their actual work. Sick days started to rise, and we had one or two resignations. All of these signs were clues that something was amiss. Something had to change.

And then, bam, Covid-19 came along and slapped us right across the face, delivering the message that we couldn't ignore these issues anymore. We couldn't afford for our people to be passive anymore. Now, more than ever, we'd have to open up our playbook and get back to what it was that made us great in the first place. We'd have to throw ourselves into the task of saving our company by making decisions we'd been putting off, and I knew the way to do this was for us to show inspirational leadership and be values-led.

The Covid-19 pandemic changed the way we work forever. We packed up our desks at the office, set ourselves up at home and had to become ring-light aficionados so we'd be well lit for our Zoom calls. We scrambled for toilet paper rolls on supermarket shelves while sporting bad hair regrowth (well, that's how my 2020 went anyway), and in doing so, the virus shook us out of our collective comfort zone. And while the tremendous suffering and hardship will never be forgotten in our generation, the virus also created an opportunity to study how we can live and work better.

Suddenly, companies that had forever said that "work-from-home doesn't work" were proven wrong. People stopped commuting, thereby gaining hours back in their day. Parents stopped having to sneak out of the office to go pick up the kids, and less important projects were put on hold.

Yes, I saw the challenges in all of this, but I saw the opportunities even more clearly. The future of work had arrived, and this was our chance to shake things up and say goodbye to an archaic system that had only really gotten us so far and left us burned out and stressed. Here was our chance to take the best parts of office life and discard the parts that had stood in the way of us truly being effective for so long: things like unrealistic working hours, unproductive meetings and all those other outdated systems of bureaucracy.

As the world changed, the way my team worked changed too. We went back to being scrappy and cutting a few corners. We became more intentional with every piece of work we did because time mattered and where we focused mattered. We forgot about roles and titles and processes. We challenged each other. Tough decisions that once would have taken weeks or months were made in minutes. We tried things just because they felt right. And you know what? We were all happier and more fulfilled for it—and not just because we didn't have to commute to an office anymore.

During the months of saving my business, *The New Hustle* was born. What started as a guide for my team gradually morphed into what I hope will be your professional bible for navigating this new world in which we find ourselves. It's a book of stories and strategies learned from my own years in the business trenches, with a side of advice from the entrepreneurs and leaders I've been lucky to spend time with over those years.

What I've learned over the years of building my companies has given me a lot to share about culture (again, "the way things are done around here") and how to get the best from your people: which, through studying and talking with our tens of thousands of Business Chicks members each year, we know is still the number one business challenge for most companies. It's the thing they bemoan across the globe each and every day. How do you find and keep amazing people? How do you get your people to be doing work that engages them each day, and how do you create an environment where people want to work? How do you get them to a point where they appreciate all you do and are grateful for having a seat on the bus? And if you're one of those people occupying a seat on that bus, how do you put forward the best version of yourself? How do your actions contribute to the business so it thrives as a supportive place for everyone? What can you do to make tackling work a pleasure and not a chore?

In his book *Start with Why*, Simon Sinek said: "over 80 percent of Americans do not have their dream job. If more knew how to build organizations that inspire, we could live in a world in which that statistic was the reverse—and over 80 percent of people loved their jobs. People who love going to work are more productive and more creative. They go home happier and have happier families. They treat their colleagues and clients and customers better. Inspired employees make for stronger companies and stronger economies."

It seems to me an important web to weave. When we work out how to build companies that engage their humans positively, then that impact has a flow-on effect to almost everyone else too—their colleagues, loved ones, customers, communities, and so the list grows.

It's my hope that *The New Hustle* becomes your handbook for how to do all this, and more. Whether you're a business owner, a team leader, or a team player, it's my aim that *The New Hustle* becomes a guide to transform the way you work and that it brings you more fulfillment and fun in your life. And as with any good game, I hope it challenges you into playing all-out, getting as absorbed and inspired as I did, and that you ultimately emerge a happier human from it.

It'd be easy to reduce *The New Hustle* into four words—*work smarter, not harder*—or classify it as a guide for working in a post-pandemic world, but that'd be over-simplifying it. This book is so much more than that. *The New Hustle* is the start of a movement for us all. It's reimagining everything you know about what it means to work well so that at the end of every day, you can look back, smile and say, "Yep, that mattered."

I truly believe a revolution has begun. This is our chance to see that there is an easier way to do things. There are shortcuts to be made. There is time to be saved. There is more fun and fulfillment to be had. The way we used to work is dead, and it's been replaced with a new way of working that can reinvigorate us all if we let it.

What this book expects of you and what you can expect from this book

Mostly, expectations are entirely shitty things. They can leave you bereft and disappointed. But every now and then, life demands you to lift your game a little, get out of your own way, do something you've never done before and be grateful that you were called to do it.

I wrote this book to provoke something in you. When you're done with it, it should be dog-eared, highlighted, written on, underlined. There should be coffee stains on some of the pages. Your bookmark might be an airline ticket because you've bought this on the way to somewhere. My hunch is that you're a person always going places, which is how this book found itself into your hands in the first place—perhaps someone recommended it to you because they know you're a seeker, always looking to improve and grow. Or perhaps it just spoke to you and you listened to that voice and bought it. Go you!

This book expects you're going to be a little or a lot changed by the time you get to the last page. It also expects you not to be lazy: that you're going to *do* some things along the way so that you *can* be a little or a lot changed by the end. I've made parts of this book super practical, so you're going to find lots of useful info within these pages to pick up and start using straightaway. Please do that.

I expect parts of this book to be a little bit confronting. It should make you a little uncomfortable. If you're reading this book and thinking, "That's amazing, but it isn't possible for me or the place I work," I hope it encourages you to step up and make the changes you want to see, or look elsewhere and find the workplace or role that's right for you. And by this, I mean that if you're not happy in work or in life, it's ultimately up to you to make a change. Remember you always have choices— you can leave a job if your employer is not supportive, or you can choose to stay and work out a plan for how you're going to get what you need. You can also allow yourself to choose finding happiness outside of work, whether that means moving, leaving a relationship, picking up that hobby you love again or just not putting so much pressure on yourself to always get things right.

If I know one thing, I know this: action is everything. Getting into action is a sure-fire way to combat most anything: being broke, being lonely, feeling funky, having your career stall, not knowing which way to turn, seeing your business plateau and so on and so on. I expect you to get into action while you're reading this book, and I expect you to be just that little bit further ahead by the time you're done.

What exactly is the new hustle?

Everywhere we turn, we're told to hustle.

Hustle until you don't have to introduce yourself. Hustle until your haters ask if you're hiring. Hustle beats talent when talent doesn't hustle. Hustle until you've built the muscle, blah blah blah. The signs on the walls of co-working spaces tell us: "Don't stop when you're tired. Stop when you're done." Our coffee mugs remind us to rise and grind, and Instagram tells us that good things come to those who just keep going.

And that they do! Great things come to those who work hard and apply themselves to their goals. These days, though, we're glorifying the wrong hustle and expecting humans to work as hard as we expect our laptops and phones to work. We're high-fiving the workers who are only living for work, and that's not cool. Being stretched, burned out and racked with stress is not a condition any human can sustain for long. There should be no gold medal for working yourself into the ground.

The problem with the traditional sense of "hustling" is that it measures input and not necessarily output. Hustling enthusiasts would have you believe in excessively long hours and limited play time, whereas I'm more interested in what you've achieved, not how much sleep you didn't get.

Don't get me wrong, I've hustled hard at many points in my life. Long nights. Early mornings. Twenty years of building and running businesses when you know no better will do that. I've been guilty of working myself into the ground, my depleted adrenals begging me to slow down on many occasions.

These days though, with six young kids, I'm simply too tired to hustle in that traditional sense. Sure, sometimes a few long nights and early mornings are still required, but for the most part, I've gotten really good at doing the right stuff quickly so that I can be present for the times that matter more than my inbox.

The life choices I've made mean I don't have the time available to me to rehearse things over and over. No matter what the project, I always try to make my work mindful and focused, rewriting my own rules about what it takes to be effective.

For me, that means less natter in the office kitchen, no long lunch breaks and turning down as many coffee catch-ups as I can get away with. I don't have the luxury to write and rewrite emails as I'd like to, or sit in a two-hour meeting and debate an issue that doesn't need to be given that amount of airtime. It also means working hard for short periods of time and having something to look forward to at the end of that period of intense work.

This kind of hustle has nothing to do with hours worked. It's about being intentional with the work you do and the way you do it. It's making soulful choices at every turn, and always gently asking the questions that make the difference—Is this filling me up? Am I growing now? Am I good at this? And the kicker—am I making life better for others?

The New Hustle is about cutting corners. It's about being spontaneous. It's about bringing more fun into your work and more life into your life. It's about being effective in everything you do, and not striving for what others want because you've become detached from what it is *you* really want. It's not spending a second longer on a task that won't really change the ultimate outcome. It's knowing when to step into hard work (and there will be times) and knowing when you can pull back and rest well.

The New Hustle is about being values-led in what you do and not being coerced or influenced away from those values. It's trusting your instincts. It means being your true self and not watering yourself down just because that's more comfortable for everyone else. It's an effort that produces the results you want and pays the dividends you deserve.

This is the kind of hustle I'm interested in, and this is the kind of hustle I want for you. And while of course we don't all have the luxury or privilege to dictate our own hours or choose exactly how we work, there are some strategies we can all learn to make life better.

Let's jump right in!

RULE #1: IS IT WORKING OR NOT WORKING?

If whatever you're doing isn't working, don't do it harder.

Martha Beck

My friend Belinda Fitzpatrick ran a super successful events business for more than seven years. She hustled in the traditional sense to get it going; her goal was always to build a business that would allow the control, creativity and flexibility she didn't think she could get from a traditional workplace. And it worked—Belinda became known in her hometown as the go-to for weddings and corporate events, and she had a long list of clients that would make anyone sit up and pay attention.

"I knew that building my business to that point was going to take a whole lot of blood, sweat and tears, but I was up for it. I was hands-on, knee-deep, and knew no other speed than a million miles per hour. I wore the frantic pace like a badge of honor."

But after an extreme case of morning sickness left her hospitalized during her first pregnancy, followed by the premature birth of her son, Belinda was challenged to make some tough calls and change the hustle she'd become accustomed to. "My ability to simply get out of bed took a battering most days, let alone my ability to run a business, lead a team and meet obligations to clients across the country," she said.

"I finally accepted that the picture of success that I had once painted for myself needed to change to suit my new circumstances . . . I understood that sharing my best self at work and at home was only going to be possible if I gave myself the space to truly be present in each setting—no more running at a million miles per hour and rushing through life."

Belinda took a long, hard look at what she wanted from her life and her work, and decided to close the business and go back to working for someone else. And the best part? She found a role with one of her most-loved clients.

"The new scenario allowed me to continue the work which brought me so much pride and fulfillment while also providing increased value and improved results for the client," she told me. "But perhaps most importantly for me, the new role allowed me to realize a new sense of happiness. I was now able to switch off once the working day was done and be truly present as the mom and wife I so desperately wanted to be."

Isn't that cool? It's a story we don't hear enough, really. There can be a lot of unnecessary shame that comes along with closing a business, and I often hear of people who consider themselves failures if it didn't work out. It takes guts to admit you need to sidestep when something isn't going the way you intended, and we need to let go of this shame and notch it up to experience, just like Belinda did.

There's a great tool I use in business and my personal life all the time. When I'm stuck with something, feeling stressed, feeling tired or feeling confused, I stop and ask myself: "Be honest—is it working, or is it not working?"

This black-and-white question takes all the emotion out of the situation and gets you into problem-solving mode. When you've got to "Nope, it's not working for me," you'll soon find yourself asking, "Okay, great, what needs to be done about it?"

Think about any areas in your life right now that may be causing you some pain or angst. Your relationship? Your performance at work? Your health and fitness? The stress of your business? Stop for a second and ask yourself honestly: "Is it working, or is it not working?"

If your answer is "No, it's not working," then make like Belinda, and do something about it.

relax.

RULE #2: TO EARN POWER, YOU MUST FIRST RELAX

You might have heard the quote: "Happiness is often the result of being too busy to be miserable."

Now I didn't write that, and no one knows for sure who did, but if I had I would have taken out the word "busy" and replaced it with the word "full," because busy is a badge of honor we need to unpin from our collars. It's become a way to define ourselves and prove our worthiness, and there's a broken social currency connected to it.

How boring is it when we ask someone how they are and they reply with, "Oh, so busy!" Parents often appear hurried and overwhelmed at the school gate, rolling their eyes at the next activity they must deliver their children to; or at the office a co-worker will complain that they're already late for their next meeting ("Sooooooo busy!") or behind on a deadline. Our default is always to dramatize how busy we are and play against one another in a game of who's busiest. Why do we keep doing this?

While we're busy telling everyone just how busy we are, it's interesting to learn that our work hours have actually been in decline and haven't increased as much as most of us think they have. For the past five decades, our work hours have flatlined at around forty hours per week. This might not be your reality, but it's the reality of many full-time workers.

Billionaire Jack Ma, who founded e-commerce giant Alibaba, says, "My grandfather worked sixteen hours a day in the farmland and thought he was very busy. We work eight hours a day, five days a week and think we are very busy."

I've got a confession to make: I'm not busy. My life is very full, and I have a heck of a lot of responsibilities, but I'm not busy. I have no interest in ever being busy again.

My friend Liz is not busy either. I mean, Liz *could* be busy—she has *New York Times* bestselling books to write (she has five of those under her belt already) and speeches to give and causes to support as well. But Liz is not busy. Nope. Far from it. The only thing Liz gets busy at is being relaxed (and I don't mean hot-stones-and-essential-oils kind of relaxed either). I'm talking about the great Elizabeth Gilbert, of course, and I love her take on what it means to let go of our obsession with busyness.

Liz says that the most powerful person in any room is the most relaxed one, and she suggests that the way to get there is to work on our priorities: that is, who—and what—are most important in our lives.

Liz isn't shy about telling people that if she doesn't get back to their emails, it's not because she's busy—it's because she doesn't care. That might sound harsh, but anyone who understands boundaries will tell you it's simply self-preservation. Don't confuse Liz's holding boundaries with her being unkind, either—she's one of the kindest people I've ever met, but she stores that kindness up for the people who matter most to her.

To me, being relaxed appears as living in the moment, having fun, breathing more, caring less about people's perceptions of you, choosing who and what really matters and occasionally grabbing the hot stones and essential oils when you can.

A busy person is consumed by perfectionism.
A relaxed person is consumed by purpose.

A busy person is good at everything.
A relaxed person is good at the important things.

A busy person complains about all they have to do.
A relaxed person lets the results of their work do
    the talking.

A busy person feels better when others are busy too.
A relaxed person wants people around them to be
    effective.

A busy person gets frustrated by many competing
priorities.

A relaxed person selects a few priorities carefully.

A busy person constantly appears rushed.

A relaxed person always appears calm.

Which type of person do you want to be?

RULE #3: DO THE RIGHT WORK

Management is doing things right;
leadership is doing the right things.

Peter Drucker

One of the core values of my company is "Do the right work,"
and I'm not ashamed to say we stole it. I first saw this on the wall
of a company we were visiting on one of our Knowledge + Study
Tours to Los Angeles. We run these tours two or three times a
year, and they've become the most phenomenal experience
for the twenty-five or so members who get to come along. We
partner up with leading business schools in LA and New York
and get to learn from some of the world's best professors and

academics. We also get to experience some money-can't-buy activities like going behind the scenes at Disneyland or learning how to lead through pressure and stress with the Fire Department of New York (hint: amazing!).

All of these experiences are incredible, but in my mind, the best parts of these tours are the brilliant businesses that open their doors for us to learn from. On one tour we were able to spend time with TechStyle Fashion Group—a company with a bunch of brands such as Fabletics (which Kate Hudson co-founded) and ShoeDazzle under their umbrella. TechStyle is an online subscription fashion retailer with more than five million VIP members. In 2019, they surpassed $750 million in revenue. They've had an incredible trajectory, and when we asked their execs how they managed to achieve this growth, a number of them pointed to their core values as being central to this success.

The core value I loved the most (and subsequently stole for our business) was "Do the right work," as it's a problem I see companies and individuals suffering from all the time: they run around being busy but without actually achieving much in the process. Sure, they're working hard, but they're often busy doing the wrong work.

It's worth mentioning that "Do the right work" matters as much in our homes as it does in our workplaces. It shouldn't matter whether the house is always spotlessly clean, the dishwasher is unloaded, and the books on the shelf are color-coded (do you do that too?). What matters is that you kissed your partner when you arrived home, that you looked them in the eye at least once that day and told them you loved them, that you got on the floor and played blocks with your kids without your phone for even just five minutes or read them a book before tucking them into bed, or you spent a few moments petting the dog. It's choosing to do the activities that matter the most rather than getting busy and distracted with the ones that matter less.

In our business, doing the right work manifests in many different ways. For example, one of the ways we make money is through selling sponsorship opportunities—so brands might buy a page in our magazine, or if they're a car brand, for example, they might place one of their vehicles in the foyer at our events, or they might even partner with us by sponsoring a digital workshop we're producing. It's actually a hugely labor-intensive exercise for us as more than eighty brands a week approach us wanting to partner up, from the local yoga studio to a major credit card brand. Just to respond to each one of these requests creates a mountain of work for our sales team.

Doing the right work in this case means getting smarter and faster in choosing whom to work with. It's working out who are the tire kickers and who are the quality potential partners. We could waste a ton of valuable time talking and going back and forth and having coffees and meetings with the wrong brands, only to learn that they don't have the type of budget that we need to make a campaign happen. We've worked hard on training our team to know when to shut a conversation down (preferably very early in the process so as not to waste anyone's time) and when to invest time in the brands that could actualize into healthy, paying clients. So, doing the right work here means saying no faster (in a lovely way, of course) and concentrating on the more likely lucrative opportunities.

Only *you* will be able to know if you're spending your time doing the right work. It's different for every person and every company, but here are some general examples of wrong work and right work.

Wrong work Saying yes to every person who asks to have a coffee with you.

Right work Strategically building a relationship with someone who you know can help you and who you can help in return, and then working to foster that relationship.

Wrong work Starting an email chain to five people about a problem that then turns into a mammoth game of email tennis with everyone throwing in their two cents' worth.

Right work Identifying the decision maker and picking up the phone and sorting out the problem as fast as possible.

Wrong work If you're in sales, agreeing to a meeting with someone without knowing their budget, or without at least doing your research well enough to know if they're a potential fit.

Right work Clarifying their budget before meeting; if that's not possible, pre-qualifying to the best of your abilities.

Wrong work Starting a business and focusing your time on producing a podcast, designing your business cards and perfecting your look on Instagram. Of course, for some businesses this might be a necessary or wise strategy, but for most, these tasks can be built over time and usually shouldn't be the priority.

Right work Finding paying clients who can start giving you solid income and doing all you can to look after them.

Wrong work Micro-managing your team through too many meetings and conversations, thinking you need to be involved in every conceivable detail of what's happening.

Right work Hiring smart people and trusting them to do their job well.

Wrong work Jumping into a task or project without thinking about whether you're actually the one who needs to be doing it.

Right work Thinking about who could do the task or project better and delegating it to them, if that option is available to you.

Wrong work Spending too much time in your inbox, mindlessly looking for something to respond to or answering every email that comes in when it comes in.

Right work Setting aside two (or three if you must) sessions in the day to check and respond to your emails.

RULE #4: ASK "WHAT FOR?"

If the reason for doing something is that everyone else
is doing it, it's not a good enough reason.

Warren Buffett

We've been trained that when it comes to business, bigger is better. Business owners take delight in bragging about all the new hires they're taking on and how their company is growing, growing, growing. They celebrate as their revenue rises and their team doubles. With this growth comes all sorts of fresh challenges—how to retain culture as it was designed originally, how to remain efficient, how to find talent to fill all the new roles—and before you realize what's happening, you're managing people, problems and processes rather than building your business. The irony of growth is that you're often making less money than you were before while having to deal with more problems. Less money, more problems.

The same pattern can be found in the pursuit of a bigger career. I'm sure we can all think of examples of people who strive to climb the corporate ladder, mindlessly chasing the next promotion and the next pay raise, without ever asking themselves what they are actually aiming to achieve.

Sometimes I think we chase the wrong things just because we believe it's what we're meant to do. We're told to get a job with more responsibility, and we're told we need to get promoted because that's what everyone else does. I have a couple of people in my organization who are great leaders but have no ambition of managing more team members. I'm one of them!

A salesperson might be great at selling and feel as though they have to strive for the next rung on the career ladder by becoming the sales manager. After all, being the sales manager most likely comes with a higher salary and perhaps some more prestige, and it might make them feel a little more proud at a barbecue when people ask what they do for a living. The problem is that in most companies, when salespeople shift into being the boss or the manager of a team of sales executives, their role changes from rainmaking, hunting down leads and chasing deals into hours and hours of meetings and reports and administration. There's no problem with this if you enjoy these activities and thrive on making sure they're done well, but most great salespeople aren't built for desk roles and would rather be out there inspiring others and closing deals.

I've found it very useful to ask myself (and my colleagues, frustratingly at times, no doubt) two little words before starting any task or project. The two little words are: "What for?" Sometimes we do things mindlessly for the sake of doing them. We're going through the motions, and instead of being intentional and smart with our time and what we're trying to achieve, we just do the same things over and over with no real outcome or effect.

So someone in my team will say, "We need more video content," and I'll ask, "What for?" to encourage some intelligent and robust discussion. Sometimes there's no real purpose or need to do the tasks we choose to do. We just do them because we think they need to be done, and it's considered a good idea at the time. Now, of course, every single business's requirements are going to be different, and what is a priority for us might not be a priority for you. I get it, but just because everyone else is investing a ton in video doesn't mean we need to, unless it specifically works for us and returns what we need it to return.

In a business sense, it's about knowing *why* you do things and being brave enough to really question your activities all the time. It's about never settling with an answer of: "Well, everyone else is doing it, so we should too," or "We just thought it might be a good idea." Coming back to the "What for?" question and encouraging that same level of curiosity in your people is a really important skill for any smart leader to master.

Of course, the "What for?" question isn't just for managers, the C-suite or business owners. Any strong leader will appreciate a team member who stops and says, "Actually, I've thought of a better idea for tackling this."

When the pandemic hit, the question "What for?" became even more critical to my company's survival. We had no choice but to get back to being scrappy. For the people who love layers of process and management and procedure and systems and meetings, this idea was sheer terror. For me, it was like coming home. It was a return to our deeply entrepreneurial roots. When the virus started to take hold and a ban on in-person events was put into place, a massive percentage of our livelihood was swept away. We had to put tools down, get the whiteboard out and strategize ourselves into a new hustle if we were to survive.

The big management consulting companies might argue against this, but when it comes down to it there are really only two ways to save a company: you can make more money, or you can cut costs. The first option had been taken away from us, so the second one it was. Go!

We interrogated every single line item on our profit and loss statement, deliberating over every detail. Could we still afford cleaners a couple of times a week for the office? No, we could not. Could we afford the many external consultants who'd advised us the past few years? No, we could not. Could we afford weekly sessions with my business coach? No, we could not. Could we afford to keep employing the number of people we were? No, we could not. Unfortunately, and inevitably, saving our company also meant cutting some jobs, which was of course the hardest decision. If we were to salvage the business and the jobs of the remaining people inside it, these tough calls had to be made.

And here's where the learnings started to appear. Almost a year after the pandemic hit and those tough calls were made, our revenue was down by over 70 percent, but so too were our expenses. And our net profit? While it wasn't what it had been in years past, it wasn't dire. As I sit here writing this book, my team is smaller. They choose whether they work from home or the office. I'm more engaged with them because there are fewer layers of management. And there's an unbreakable sense of camaraderie because together we survived this phase and have emerged stronger from it.

Marriott Hotels took the same approach and miraculously grew their net profit during the pandemic, even though their hotel rooms in the US were only a third full and in Europe only a fifth. How did they do this? Through herculean cost-slashing measures, or in other words, they saved their way through the pandemic.

There are many others who have taken the opportunity offered by the pandemic to think more deeply about the direction they were taking and whether it was really what they wanted. (Of course, some were forced into this by circumstances, others by the desire to do something different.) My friend India was laid off from her job as a personal assistant, so she took the chance to do what she'd always wanted to do but could never quite find the time for—study interior design. She admitted to me that she would never have found the courage to do this if she hadn't been made redundant. Another friend of mine, Amy, worked in a small business that got hit hard with Covid-19, losing the majority of their revenue and clients. Amy loved her job and loved the business, so she went to her manager and offered to help out more with other tasks outside of her regular job. She ended up working in two different departments during the lockdown (remotely, of course) and learned a whole heap of skills from the experience. Thankfully, the company has picked up since, and Amy is back in her old role, armed with lots of new knowledge and some serious career kudos too.

Business Chicks member Virginia Brookes recently told me, "We always dreamed of escaping the rat race, heading off traveling and moving out of the city but I was always so busy working in my life and in my business I could never look at the bigger picture."

When the pandemic hit, Virginia lost 90 percent of her business. Leading her team through the unknown began to take a toll, and she felt herself plunging into the depression she'd been diagnosed with twelve months earlier.

"I was posting videos on social media all bright and full of life, but inside I was slowly breaking down, and I could feel myself spiraling . . . I was finally at home with my kids and husband and was enjoying the time, and all I could think was I wanted to escape reality, and fulfill a long-term dream of heading off in our RV and deciding what I wanted to do with my life. I'm not afraid to say that when I headed off I almost didn't care if I came back to a business—I would just start again!"

A few months into their RV trip, Virginia felt more relaxed and present than she had in years. It was the nudge she needed to sell her house and move an hour out of the city for good. Four months later, the kids are in new schools, they collect eggs from their chickens every morning and Virginia spends two or three days a week in the office, staying in the city at a hotel sometimes so she can do two "big" days. Her team is also set up to work from home, but she says most still choose to come into the office to be around each other.

"I look back now on 2020 as the most incredible gift I could have been given—I was given permission from the universe to slow down, realign with what was really important and to make decisions with a clear head."

Makes you think, doesn't it? We can apply the "What for?" thinking to almost every situation in life, too, and it's a beautiful way to stop and think about why we're actually doing something and see if a bit of a reprogram might be required. On one of my last trips to New York, I met a lovely woman who was on vacation there and we got to talking. She told me how she had brought two empty suitcases to New York to "shop up a storm" and "buy everything she possibly could." My immediate reaction was to ask, "What for?" I mean, how many new purses do we actually need? We're often so much on autopilot and listening to the soundtrack of our past behaviors that we don't stop to really question our actions. It wasn't my place to ask this stranger, "What for?" but if you're a switched-on person wanting to get terrific results efficiently, you'll add these two little words to your vocabulary and help everyone else around you wake up too.

determine.

I call myself a career entrepreneur, and what I mean by this is that I've never really worked for anyone apart from myself. After some waitressing as a teenager, I went on to work at and then buy into a business when I was eighteen years old. Apart from these experiences, I've been self-employed my whole career. I've started and acquired a few different companies since then, but the one I've given the last sixteen years of my life to is Business Chicks. I bought that business when I was twenty-five and the wild ride continues to this day.

The experience of always working for myself means I've had to make it up as I've gone along. If there was a problem at work, I was never able to ask my boss how to handle it or what the best practice was, or rely on past experience to guide me. I simply didn't have that experience, so I learned through trying different strategies and doing what I felt made the most sense at the time.

I dropped out of college after six months when I realized it wasn't for me, so as well as being self-employed, I'm self-taught. Everything I've learned is through the books I've read, the people I've studied, the courses I've attended, the networks I've built and the chances I've taken. I've learned through hands-on problem solving, without the influences of a corporate system to tell me how things should be done. For example, when I've wanted to make a new hire, I've started by going to the people I know and asking if they know someone suitable who'd be great, instead of filling in a form, going to HR, setting up panel interviews and psychometric assessments, et cetera. I've always tried to get the best possible result in the fastest possible way, and if that means cutting some red tape and breaking a few outdated rules to get there, then so be it.

A lot of time gets wasted in the workplace because people do things the way the system tells them they should, when sometimes the system doesn't make sense and takes twice the amount of time. If you can use the "What for?" philosophy in your day-to-day practices, you'll save a lot of time and make your work way more effective. I've popped some ideas next up about where to start.

RULE #5: WELL, THAT COULD HAVE BEEN AN EMAIL

> *People who enjoy meetings*
> *should not be in charge of anything.*
>
> Thomas Sowell

I'm not exactly sure who this Thomas Sowell is, but I have a feeling we could be best friends.

How much time do you think you spend per week in ineffective meetings or on long conference calls that could likely run shorter? My guess is too much.

A 2017 study by *Harvard Business Review* found that Americans sit through 11 million meetings each day, and most leaders find them to be unproductive and demotivating.

I'm so glad I'm not the only one.

I've always been someone who prefers getting into action as opposed to talking, which is why it kills me to give hours of my day over to ineffectual meetings. Perhaps annoyingly, I'm the first one to speak up when a meeting is running off course or just becoming a talkfest.

A long time ago we decided that in our business "doing the right work" means less time spent in meetings having conversations that seem to go around in circles and more time spent making decisions and getting action items out. Poorly run and managed meetings are such killers of great culture.

To bring about this change, I had my leaders analyze how many hours they were spending and their teams were spending in meetings each week. And then I got one of our operations people to calculate how much those meetings were costing us based on the hourly rate of each of the staff members involved. The time that people spent in meetings came back as somewhere between ten hours a week and two days per week for our more senior team members—eek! Based on those figures, the meetings turned out to be very expensive. One administrative meeting we used to hold cost us over $9,500 each time, and I can tell you that we most certainly didn't get $9,500 back in value!

Apart from being costly and demotivating (I mean, have you ever heard someone exclaim, "Yippee! I have a meeting now!"), here are six reasons why meetings can suck and what to do about it.

No one is really leading it I'm sure we've all been in plenty of meetings where no one has "officially" been assigned full accountability or has been given the power to run it effectively. When I first started out in my career, I joined an entrepreneurs' network in which I'd meet up with seven other entrepreneurs in my group for three hours each month. One of my peers ran this meeting—and she was hard-core! She'd never let us go over our allocated time, and there was a process for policing us if we did. The discipline was amazing, and because the culture had been set that it was acceptable for her to act this way, we all expected it and were on the same page. Did it feel uncomfortable at times? It sure did, but we all had a good sense of humor and appreciated our time not being wasted. Did this rigor mean the meetings were always effective? Hell, yeah!

There's no specific reason for the meeting I've seen leaders insist on having one-on-ones with their team members each week, and it can descend into a waste of time very quickly. If you don't have a relationship where you can grab each other for five minutes a couple of times a day, I'd say you don't have a good relationship. I'm all for banking up discussion points and not bothering each other every single time something comes up, but spending an hour or two in a one-on-one is very counter-productive unless there's a big problem you need to work through. Managers should know what their people are working on, where they're stuck and what their roadblocks are; they should be helping them throughout the week in some sort of effective process that they co-design, not sitting in a small room shooting the breeze just because it has a placeholder in the calendar each week. Employees should also be given the power to be able to say, "You know what? I'm all good, I don't need a catch-up this week." The problem is that lots of managers feel this is what they're meant to be doing in order to be seen as a good manager. A good manager empowers and trusts people to get on with their work without the need to be micro-managed and have every conceivable detail discussed.

People bring their phones into the meeting A while back, we mandated the "no phones in meetings" policy, and it's now become a habit to not to bring them at all. Of course, we appreciate that there are times when it's necessary to have your phone right by you, but for the most part you should try to give your full attention to your colleagues and what's being decided on. (I once had a guy come into a meeting with me and ask if it was okay if he kept his phone out, as his wife was three days overdue with their baby and he wanted to be available for her. Um, of course! There are valid, meaningful exceptions to this rule, an overdue baby definitely being one.) Build a reputation as the person who doesn't have their phone with them in meetings, and if you must bring it in, make sure it's for a solid reason and make sure you share that reason with the group (where appropriate, of course).

The meeting length is dictated by the calendar Think about it . . . why do we always book meetings in half hour or hour blocks and start them exactly on the hour or half hour? It's just because we've been trained to do that. You don't need to fill the space or pad out the time if the meeting is done. Yep, you might have booked it from 2 to 3 p.m., but there's no reason why time has to expand to fill that slot. It can be a good idea to start each meeting with a reminder of that, too: "Hopefully we can wrap this up a little earlier and get back to our day" could be a lovely phrase to use here.

When I was running my staffing agency in my twenties, we used to start the day with a "daily huddle" where we'd all stand around and discuss what our focus was for the day and if we had any roadblocks that we needed to talk about. This daily huddle would kick off at 8:37 a.m. sharp. It sent a message to the team to be ready by then and also meant we got ourselves organized beforehand, buying us a few more minutes than if we'd started at say 8:45 a.m. The weirdness worked.

The meetings take more than two pizzas to feed the room At Amazon they believe that less is more. They live by a rule that each meeting should be small enough that its attendees can be fed with two pizzas. Kind of genius. Big meetings can be the worst time thieves ever known to the human race.

There's a bunch of people in the meeting who don't need to be there I do try to dial in to our company-wide meeting each Tuesday. It's conducted via video conference as we have so many people working remotely now. I love hearing the updates from all the different departments and connecting with the team, but there's also a point at which I add no value and also don't need to know what's being discussed. We generally end these meetings with an update from our operations team, and the discussion heads into topics I really don't need to know about. When this starts to happen, I'll begin waving at the screen and go, "Okay, team, I'm out! I don't need to know this stuff, but love you all and chat soon!" Perhaps the first couple of times I did this I might have appeared a little cold or as if I didn't care, but if my job as the leader of the business is to set the pace on productivity and effectiveness, then this seems a good place to start.

Steve Jobs was known for throwing out participants who didn't need to be in the room. Elon Musk is famous for walking out when he's no longer required. He once said, "It is not rude to leave. It is rude to make someone stay and waste their time." It's nothing personal—these guys just recognized the importance and value of time and spending it wisely.

If your meetings could do with a makeover, here are some ideas for getting them back on track.

Change up the setting Do you meet in the same spot every time? Try moving the location of the meeting to inject some fresh energy into it. Also have people mix up where they sit and who they sit next to. Or take the initiative yourself and sit down next to someone new or who you'd really like to get to know.

Don't take meetings without an agenda If there are no pressing items on the agenda, then cancel the meeting altogether. Facebook's COO Sheryl Sandberg is known for coming into meetings with a spiral-bound notebook filled with the items that need to be talked about. As each of them gets discussed, she crosses them off. If this takes only half of the allocated meeting time, then the meeting ends. This is a really clear strategy for keeping meetings succinct and on track. The same goes for meeting attendance—ask for clarity about what's on the agenda before even accepting.

Make the meetings smaller Make like Amazon and downsize your meetings. In the same way smaller companies enjoy overall higher engagement from their people, smaller meetings invite greater participation and more engagement from their attendees. When you have fewer people attending your meetings, there's a greater opportunity for everyone to feel as if they're personally responsible for what was discussed. We've all sat in huge meetings before and thought, "Someone else will take care of that," or worse, been confused as to what was actually decided (if anything!).

Communicate lots If you need to lead or influence a shift in meeting culture in your company, be sure to clearly communicate why the shift needs to happen. Be gentle but firm about how things are going to improve in case people feel put out by not being invited to meetings they were regularly let into. (If this is you, just think about all the extra time you'll have. But if you continue to be invited to regular meetings that aren't relevant to you, persuade the meeting organizer to cut you a break.)

Get rid of the weekly meetings Even if you get the chance to change your weekly meeting to once every two weeks, you'll instantly save a bunch of time. A manager who had nine direct reports once told me how she had become disengaged with her work because of the number of meetings she had to hold with her team. She decided to change her weekly one-on-ones to fortnightly meetings. To ensure the team still felt supported, she started an "office hours" session each week for her team where she made herself completely available to them for whatever they needed. She found that mostly they didn't even use this time, but it was there in her calendar in case they did. Between her and her team, they've saved hours of time each week, and she's feeling far more engaged in her role now. I bet her team are too! If you're on the team and your manager is still insisting on the status quo, perhaps you could point out the amount of time that everyone would save.

If you've organized an online meeting, insist that participants have their cameras on Just make this one a mandatory rule. There's nothing worse than being on a Zoom call with half the participants' cameras turned off. Are they even there? Are they listening? Are they interested in what you have to say? Make sure that if you're the one setting the online meeting, you let all attendees know beforehand that this will be a "cameras-on" meeting. Not being present and truly showing up for an online meeting is as rude as checking your phone during an offline one.

Try having your meetings standing up or walking around the block Meetings where you stand or where you take a walk bring fresh energy to conversations and always lessen the amount of time it takes to get through whatever it is that needs to be discussed. Try them—they work!

Of course, all this really only applies if you are the person running the meeting, but even as a participant there is much you can do to make sure your meetings are productive. First, come prepared with necessary information on the content that will be discussed. There is nothing worse than sitting around waiting for someone to find an important set of figures or a key file. Take time before the meeting to figure out what answers you want to get from it—again, ask yourself, "What for?"—so that you can ask the right questions. There's no point sitting through a meeting if you aren't prepared to contribute, ask questions, share insights or offer to take on tasks.

Remember meetings are also a chance to learn more about the business and your colleagues—don't be afraid to reach out to someone in an area of the business that interests you, or to set up a separate time to ask for advice or counsel.

And finally, for the sake of getting back some hours in your day, try scheduling in a recurring "no meetings" day. Blocking out one day a week when you're not distracted from your work and can give 100 percent focus to ploughing through your projects and priorities can be a game changer for productivity.

Lots of my team have told me they relish their no-meetings days as they'll often work from home in their pajamas and not have to think about how they present themselves. Creating this relaxed day gives them the freedom to ideate and daydream a little, too.

RULE #6: MAKE SPACE

On the subject of daydreaming, this culture of always being "on" and busy has distracted us from thinking time, which decreases our creativity. Staying in the cycle of busy means there's no space for anything else to flourish. Every now and then, train yourself to go for a walk without your phone. Go to a café without your laptop. If you must, take a notepad and pen. Even better, take nothing at all so you can let your mind wander.

Years ago, Spanx founder Sara Blakely discovered that her best thinking happens in the car. It was on a car trip more than twenty years ago now that she came up with her brand name, pulling over to write "Spanx" on a piece of scrap paper. These days, Blakely lives too close to the Spanx headquarters to allow herself much time to think on the way to work, but she's famous for feigning "fake commutes" driving around Atlanta to create space to think creatively. She's been quoted as saying, "I live really close to Spanx, so I've created what my friends call my 'fake commute,' and I get up an hour early before I'm supposed to go to Spanx, and I drive around aimlessly in Atlanta so that I can have my thoughts come to me." Genius!

RULE #7: MAKE BETTER DEALS

I realized that I spent more time thinking
about my problem clients than my great clients.
I had to stop feeding the drama of the problem clients—
and other problems in my life.

Bonnie St. John

We've all had that client who takes up our time and makes our lives difficult. When an email arrives from them, you take a sharp inhale of breath and think, "What now?" and your mind goes to the worst possible scenario.

In the spirit of making better deals, it might be a good time to think about whether these folks are worth gently divorcing so your effort can be focused elsewhere. "But how will I replace them?" I hear you asking. I've always found that once my energy is freed up and I'm no longer spending valuable time worrying about difficult people, I've been able to focus on attracting better quality customers that I actually like working with. After all, it's true that who you say no to determines who you can say yes to.

Last year, I got approached exactly 274 times to be an "ambassador" of some sort. My team members know that figure because we track every single pitch we get sent in a Google doc. Out of those 274 potential deals, I accepted a total of three.

These pitches ranged from "I have a new tan brand—will you promote it?" to "Will you be an ambassador for xyz vodka company?" or "Can I send you an eyebrow pencil and you can post about it?" Some were asking me to promote their products and services for free, and some were offering to pay well. We considered each one of these deals carefully, but ultimately my strategy is to make a few better deals that feel right, and not make hundreds of mediocre ones that don't. The thinking with this strategy is that I can wholeheartedly give my time and efforts to a select few that I'm happy to work very hard for (and in turn I get rewarded well, too), instead of spreading myself thin across lots of brands and only being able to do an average job for them (and being paid less, of course). This strategy also means I maintain complete authenticity, as I end up only selecting brands that I'm passionate about.

When I first started Business Chicks, I was positive I needed to start with the big guns. If I could get a couple of really good brands on board, then I knew it'd be easier to attract similar quality deals. I approached one of the largest banks in the country and convinced them that we were worth partnering with. It took me more time to get that one across the line than it would have to get a bunch of smaller clients, but ultimately it proved to be a brilliant strategy. And once they were on board, it meant other strong brands started to take notice. Had I started with the beauty salon down the road, it would have taken me ten more years to work up to the caliber of that huge bank. I guess it's about backing yourself and ultimately finding the confidence that you're worth it. You're definitely worth at least trying for those deals.

Now even if you do not have the power to make strategic decisions like this in your workplace—to pick and choose your customers or partners—there's still lots you can do to make sure the deal you get at work is the one you really want. Even if it does mean some delicate negotiation.

Making better deals is not just about making more money. It's about being able to enjoy your work more, and it's about being able to truly work smarter and not harder. Sometimes to make a better deal you just need to be a bit more creative and think of alternative ways to structure it. Making better deals means we free up our time enormously.

This example might seem unattainable and inaccessible for us mere mortals, but the idea is worth exploring. It's widely reported that back in 2015, Beyoncé performed at a corporate event for Uber. Her usual fee would have been in the $6 million region, but instead of being paid cash, she requested to be paid in Uber stock. At the time, Uber was a private company, but in mid-2019 the company went public. The stocks have since dropped in value, but if Beyoncé had played her cards right and sold when they were at their height, she could have made herself a cool $9 million.

In a similar move, when she headlined at music festival Coachella, aside from earning a fee reported to be between $4 million and $8 million, Beyoncé also negotiated the exclusive rights to footage of the event, which was later sold to Netflix as part of a three-part series for $60 million. That's some hefty leverage right there and a great example of making a better deal.

Neither of these stories has been officially verified, but even so, there's something we can learn from this way of thinking, right?

My friend Marnie has a slightly fractious relationship with her business partner, who's considered a very difficult person by lots of people around him. Negotiating anything with him has been known to regularly end in tears and a march out of his office with no real resolution for either party. Marnie wanted to renegotiate her package (despite being the co-founder of their company) and knew her business partner wouldn't be receptive to this idea. Knowing that heading in there and simply requesting more money would be met with a firm "no way," Marnie got creative. Her role within the business was as chief rainmaker with their clients. She'd brought huge deals to the business and had run and grown the sales team effectively for the past ten years. She knew she was good at sales, and she knew she got results. So she suggested a deal that was foolproof for him and for her: pay her no salary from here on in, and simply pay a commission on the clients she brought in. He couldn't say no, as it was also in his best interests for her to bring in as much money as possible to the business. Marnie's business partner is no dummy, and after a bit of questioning and lots of back-and-forth on what the commission structure would look like, they shook hands and Marnie walked away much happier. It's been a whole year since she renegotiated her agreement, and she's been successful with further growing the company's sales. She told me she's never felt more motivated to show her business partner what she can achieve, and as a result, she's bringing in more clients and now earning almost double the amount that she was receiving before.

Next time you're negotiating, could you consider something similar to the above story? Or work in a performance bonus based on certain milestones if your boss won't give you a pay raise? Or negotiate to work on a freelance or remote basis if you really can't stand working in the office or have other responsibilities that would make working from home much easier?

Knowing what good deals and great clients look like for you and your particular circumstances is an essential element of any strong business. I'm constantly surprised that after twenty years in business I still catch my team measuring the wrong things when it comes to making good deals. It's natural for us to slip into ineffective ways from time to time, falling into the activities that are less profitable or putting too much time into work that might pay well overall but ultimately costs us more to execute.

Sometimes we get lured into the final price of a deal and don't take the time to do the work of really understanding whether it's worth our while or not. Being able to break down a client's project and understand if it makes sense to carry it out is a useful exercise worth undertaking. A great place to start is to work out what your time is worth per hour and then do the same for anyone else on your team or in the broader business. If you can then estimate the number of hours a client's project will take, you'll have a simple metric to work out whether your margins are healthy. This is a really rudimentary exercise, and of course there are more sophisticated methods, but if you follow this discipline with all your projects you'll soon start to see patterns as to what's a good deal and what's not.

This is a bit of advice I wish I'd known when starting out and is particularly relevant if you're involved in a start-up yourself or working as a sole owner. It's one thing to have work coming in, but not if you're working every hour in the day for a measly few dollars.

And don't rest on your laurels if you're employed on a regular salary. Ask around and check out some of the comparison sites out there to make sure you're getting the best possible deal for your role, your experience and your talents. Your boss is highly unlikely to point out that they're paying you bargain basement rates. It's up to you to do your homework!

Making better deals will take on an entirely different meaning for every business and every person, but ultimately it means we end up doing the work that feels better and that we enjoy doing. It's tempting to employ the thinking "I'll just start somewhere and work my way up to better clients and better deals as I go," but there's something wonderful about backing yourself into better deals right from the get-go.

RULE #8: KNOW WHEN 80 PERCENT IS ENOUGH

There are details that matter and details that don't. For each person and each business this is going to be different.

Here's an example of the details that matter in our business. Before every major event, our team agonizes over which songs we're going to play at that event. To us, the music and the mood we set matters. I once spent a whole two hours in a huge empty auditorium with just me, a couple of audio-visual guys, our DJ and two of our events producers. We were going through the rehearsal for one of our huge conferences, making sure we had the right opening track and that we perfectly timed the opening of the doors when everyone would enter the event. The whole moment needed to have the maximum amount of impact. I wanted to know that the stage curtains would open at exactly the right part of the song and that the lighting would be perfect too. Why is all this important? Because this experience forms the first impression many people have of the event, and because these details matter.

There will be priorities that need your utmost attention to detail, and it's worth taking some time to think about the areas you really need to be picky about.

That said, there is an important flipside to this thinking, and it's brought to us by marketing guru and author Seth Godin. Years ago, Seth wrote a blog post about productivity that I thought was so good I saved it. I refer back to it all the time, particularly when I'm working with a team member who I feel is getting lost in perfectionism.

In the post, he wrote about the correlation between the time we spend tweaking and perfecting our work and the actual results we get: "We spend more time worrying about the cover than we spend writing the book, more energy answering the trolls than serving our best customers, more money on concealer and blush than on healthy food."

Seth makes the point that "80 percent might be more than enough," and that less time spent on the shiny details might mean more time achieving results.

I'm always trying to encourage my team to believe in this way of thinking where it's appropriate, because striving for perfection in our work takes away the opportunity of doing more elsewhere. Whenever a newbie starts in my company, I offer my time to them to help in whatever way I can. Being able to spend this time with them also helps me get a handle on where they sit on the chasing perfection scale.

Luisa took me up on this one. A few days into her new role she called and said, "Can I have some help with responding to an email?" We had a short chat about the situation, and I gave her some coaching and then passed on the clincher to her: "Okay, so I want you to write your response in five minutes or less and blind copy me in so I know it's been done in time. Are you brave?" Luisa told me she was up for the challenge, and five minutes later my inbox pinged with her response to the client.

I called her straightaway and congratulated her on an amazing effort. She laughed and said that my style was a little unconventional, admitting that she most likely would have sat there for the best part of the next hour to try to get the response perfect. "See!" I told her. "I just gave you fifty-five minutes back in your day. You're welcome!"

A perfect, perfect email response? Worthy of only 80 percent of your time. A strong first impression for your customers? That one's worth the whole two hours in an empty auditorium.

RULE #9: IT'S OKAY TO CUT CORNERS

The other day I asked one of my team members for some data I knew she had access to. A few days later a very elaborate and impressive PowerPoint presentation hit my inbox. I could see she'd gone to great lengths to really apply herself to the task and present the numbers in a beautiful way, and I could also see that this would have taken her quite a bit of time.

While I was impressed at her design sense and commitment to the job, I also felt a little bit sheepish, because what a waste of time! All that really mattered was the data—I just needed to eyeball it, not see it wrapped up in a beautiful package. I was to blame as I should have said, "Just bullet-point it in a quick email to me, and don't spend any time on it!" but it was a great lesson for both of us in where time can be best spent.

There are corners you can cut in business—making an internal report a little less snazzy to save a few hours that can be better spent on other activities; bullet-pointing an email instead of writing a seven-paragraph essay; sticking a Post-it Note on your colleague's computer with a routine phone message instead of emailing them like you're supposed to. All of these things won't make much of a difference to the bigger picture, and you're perfectly within your rights to cut these corners from time to time.

RULE #10: STEP AWAY FROM THE TASK

The biggest mistake I see with most business owners is that they spend their time doing things they don't need to do. They get busy doing the tasks that can be outsourced to others, which of course comes at a cost, but it frees them up to be more effective elsewhere. The constant distraction of trying to do too much means they're chasing their tail and getting stressed and burned out without making any more money. This is the old hustle, and it's a vicious cycle.

I've watched the rise of personal branding over the past ten years with a lot of curiosity. While I believe that building your personal brand can have enormous upside and potential for your business or career in the most part, there are lots of instances where it can just be a distraction and become a total waste of time.

If your reason for doing activities that build your personal profile is to make more sales or build credibility with the hope to make more future sales, then 100 percent go for it. But if the "What for?" isn't strong enough, think twice. Let's say you're a mortgage broker, and your main business need is to build your sales pipeline and get a really strong list of potential customers: then holding an event where you share your "top ten tips for paying off your mortgage in the next ten years" could yield excellent results for you. If you can get twenty people in a room and they get to listen to your expertise and begin to see you as a subject matter expert, then that's gold—provided you work out a way to keep in touch with them and really maximize the opportunity, of course.

However, I've seen lots of people invest a lot of time and money into personal branding activities when it's really not needed for their type of business. Recently I met a woman called Cynthia, who runs a mystery shopping company for a specific category of clients: restaurant owners. On most nights of the week, Cynthia sends her mystery shoppers into her clients' restaurants to critique the service, the food, the amenities, cleanliness, ambience and any other useful data and observations they can collect. Cynthia then reports back to the owners on the findings. It's a very worthwhile exercise for her clients, the restaurateurs, who learn a lot about what they're doing right and where they're falling short. Over the past twenty years, Cynthia has focused on chains of restaurants, so her main contact could be someone at the head office of, say, a pizza chain. This again adds huge value as she can compare the store's findings against the other restaurants within the same chain.

Cynthia was explaining to me that her greatest need right now was to get more clients. When I asked her how she planned on doing this, she said her next marketing move was to start a podcast and get on the speaking circuit. I asked her (gently of course, changing up the words a little but with the exact same sentiment), "What for?" Her response was that podcasts were really popular, and that speaking is a good way for her to get known "in the industry." The problem is that for Cynthia's business, she doesn't need to reach a mass audience and get known to lots of people. She told me that there are probably less than 200 potential customers that she'd really want to work with in her "industry" (large restaurant chains). For Cynthia, investing in a podcast—the production fees, her time in the studio, working on a keynote or speaking career—is futile. It's a distraction from the tasks that actually get her new clients and sales. It might feel good for her ego to be able to say, "I have a podcast" or "I just went and gave a talk," but it's likely not going to get her a huge number of new clients. She'd be far better off putting her resources into systematically getting to know those 200 potential customers and working out ways to target them effectively, rather than hoping that they'll randomly listen to her podcast or happen to be at the conference she's addressing.

When I spent a little time digging deeper with Cynthia, she admitted that the only reason she was thinking this way was that everyone else was doing it, and it seemed to be the next frontier in terms of marketing. Of course, she was right in a sense, but these channels are only useful to you if they achieve your objectives and don't distract you from actually going out there and getting new clients.

So how do you stop being spread so thin and start getting into the work that really matters? You begin by building the discipline to resist doing the things that are taking you away from your more meaningful work. The solution is yours to figure out, but the goal remains the same: focus on the tasks that matter and will make a difference to your business growth.

RULE #11: MAKE HARD DECISIONS FASTER

Sometimes the hardest thing
and the right thing are the same.

Unknown

A few years back I had an opportunity to partner up with a high-profile founder. We had several initial conversations with their team, and I'd flown some of my people in for the discovery phase too. It was all really exciting, and there was definitely mutual respect and a meeting of minds between our two teams. After months of refining the offering and stress-testing the product to suit the local market, we had almost arrived at a final term sheet and were ready to pull the trigger. At this point, I was having very regular conversations with their main advisors and financiers, as they were about to invest a significant amount of cash and we needed to make sure every single detail was covered.

After months of very positive interactions, however, the tables seemed to turn. I was hearing from their senior financial people that the backer investing in me wanted to change key details of our agreement, renegotiating bits of the deal that we all thought had been well and truly signed off on months prior. I was a little confused but asked all the right questions and pressed on in good faith. The conversations continued to surprise me, though, and I started to wonder whether these were the right partners for me. What had started out as a very positive and exciting proposition was now feeling like a lot of hard work for all the wrong reasons.

Instead of trying to tackle this over emails and telephone conversations here and there, I asked if I could come in to clear up some of the confusion I was sensing. I found myself in their boardroom experiencing a very different feeling that I couldn't quite name, but it soon became clear that a hard decision had to be made.

I have no real statistic on this, but I bet you something like 95 percent of people would still have taken the deal that was on the table. It was lucrative, and these people were very influential. The extraordinary opportunity to work together was not lost on me, but now it was not sitting well. Right there and then (they didn't see it coming at all—I got the feeling no one had ever said no to them), I very politely said that I wouldn't be progressing. They were shocked, of course, but I left with my head held high, collapsing into tears as soon as I'd gotten back into my car to start the journey home. I called a friend to tell him what I'd done and remember him saying, "Wow, you're amazing. You have bigger balls than any man I know." I'm not sure that his comment was comforting at the time, but what he was trying to convey was that I'd been really brave and had just made a very significant decision.

Call me ruthless, but I'm the type of person that can't unsee a decision once I've made up my mind to make it. There's no stopping me: I simply have to honor what feels right and get it done. I see a lot of people struggling to make difficult decisions, whether that's letting go of someone in their team who isn't working out performance-wise or just might be a completely wrong cultural fit, or choosing to leave a job or relationship when it's clear it's reached its use-by date.

Overthinking robs us of so much and decreases our ability to make strong decisions. When we overthink, we get doubtful, and this wastes valuable time and makes us lose confidence in our ability to make the right decision. So how do we learn to make hard decisions faster?

The first step is to get clarity on whatever it is that you actually want. Getting out of your head and into your heart is a really useful step. If you're really clear about what you want, decisions become much easier to make. In the previous example, I was really clear on what I brought to the agreement; if there was any doubt on my investors' behalf about my ability to deliver, then I was out. I was seeking, more than any money they were going to give me, to gain their complete trust and faith in my commitment to the project. When they showed a little bit of doubt, I knew I couldn't take it any further.

We should also learn not to make decisions based on what we *think* we should do. Sometimes the way we've been brought up or the stories we tell ourselves are so strong that we forget we have the right to choose. I had a friend who was feeling stuck in her marriage and really uninspired. Her parents were still married, even though she said they probably shouldn't be given that they were both so unhappy, but they believed in the sanctity of marriage above all else and nothing was about to change. Still, this woman found herself considering whether she should get a divorce or stay in her marriage, and she just couldn't get past what her parents would think. Ironically, when she did finally leave the marriage, her elderly parents supported this decision, even saying that they'd always thought her ex-husband (as lovely as he was) wasn't right for her.

Similarly, another friend confided in me about how she couldn't stand her job. She'd taken it on a whim after being lured by the new company for a small pay increase, and after only four months in the role she realized she'd made a big mistake. She was worried about the stigma attached to leaving a job less than a year after she'd started, but knew she couldn't face a day longer there. She resigned and got her old job back, and now laughs about finding that the grass is indeed not always greener where you think it might be.

If you're someone who struggles to make big decisions in your life, it can be helpful to start practicing with smaller ones. Instead of spending half an hour scrolling through the endless options on Netflix, give yourself five minutes to decide. Do the same when you're ordering dinner in a restaurant. Being more decisive is a skill we can all master, but it takes practice to build your decision-making capabilities.

Discovering that things need to change or admitting that a situation needs to be better and then actually getting into action takes a lot of courage. Hats off to anyone willing to try!

RULE #12: LEARN HOW TO SAY NO

My goal now is to remember every place I've been, only do things I love, and not say yes when I don't mean it.

Sandra Bullock

One of the most critical skills we need to ace is learning to say no and saying it quickly. When we lack the ability to say no, so much time gets wasted. We don't only waste our own time, but we also waste other people's time—and that's a sure-fire way to create frustration and roadblocks within a team. Who of us hasn't been frustrated by the chronic indecision of someone when all we want is a yes or no answer?

I once worked alongside a manager who found it very difficult to say no. Someone would pitch a very average idea to her, and instead of shutting it down immediately (in a kind and compassionate way, of course), she'd say, "Okay, let me think about it." (Which by the way is a terrible response because it gives hope to the person suggesting the average idea that you might actually be considering it.) This manager would then go away and think about the average idea for far too long. Once she'd thought about it, she still wouldn't have decided which way to turn, so she'd invite the person in for a talk about their average idea. Again, wrong move. They'd discuss the average idea (bye-bye valuable, productive time that could have been better spent elsewhere), and at this stage, the person with the average idea would be thinking had a chance. When all this was said and done, the manager still had to make a decision, and when she'd finally land on a no (the right answer to any average idea), she'd invariably frustrate the other person as they'd been strung along for ages. I used to watch this behavior happen over and over again when it could have been avoided with a strong, "Thanks so much, but this is not for us. Please feel free to send any other ideas in the future, though!"

So how do we learn to say no without offending others? There are some great strategies, which I'll share with you in a moment, but I also think it's important to start out with the right mindset: you cannot, and never will, be responsible for another person's happiness, and it's not up to you to manage their feelings. It's up to you to manage your boundaries and your time and your workload, and there's a way to do this effectively and respectfully (but yeah, let's agree you're not a jar of Nutella, okay?).

One of the best ways to say no is to make sure that your tone remains positive and add something complimentary. So you might say, "This sounds like an incredible opportunity for the right person, but it's not for me. I really appreciate you thinking of me, though!" or "I love the sound of this for a bunch of reasons but it doesn't fit into our current strategy, so we'll pass this time but thanks so much for bringing it to my attention."

Another option is to give a reason (this can be as specific or as vague as you like) as to why you're turning down a request. You might say, "I really appreciate you asking, but I am already at capacity with my workload and can't take another project on right now," or "I'm grateful you've thought of me, but I'm on deadline with a couple of key projects right now that have to take priority."

Another great way of saying no, yet still being perceived as courteous and positive, is by offering an alternative to the request. So if you get offered a role or a new opportunity but aren't interested and know someone else who might be, you'd get a gold star for saying, "Oh thanks so much for thinking of me for this! Sounds amazing, but I'm not actively looking for my next challenge at the moment. I can, however, think of a great ex-colleague of mine who might fit your needs perfectly—would you be interested in a connection to her?" Or if you're invited into a meeting you can't make at a specific time but want to offer an alternative slot, this could work: "Oh gosh! I really want to join, but I have another call with a client slated for then. Is there any chance you could shift the meeting to either 10:30 a.m., 2 p.m. or 4 p.m. tomorrow or Thursday when I can make myself free? If so, I'll definitely make myself available for you." This sounds a lot more enthusiastic and friendly than a "Sorry, can't. Have a meeting on then already." Being helpful and offering alternatives (while still saying no to the original request and holding your boundaries) can be a great way to build your reputation and still get your needs met.

Saying no is an essential skill we all need to learn in our careers (and at home!), and the good news is that the more you say no, the better you become at it. I promise you'll buy back hours in your week and save your relationships in the process.

I've always found that if you say no in the right way, people will forgive you and understand. Waste their time and string them along, though, and you're going to be crafting a very different reputation for yourself.

bend.

We still expect women to work like they don't have kids
and raise kids like they don't work.

Amy Westervelt

Sometimes we're so used to something, we forget to interrogate why we're going along with it in the first place. A great example of this is the work hours that most workplaces accept as normal.

Emily Ballesteros is a burnout management coach, and in late 2019 she made a TikTok video about why the eight-hour workday no longer makes any sense. In the video she explained that the forty-hour work week was a concept introduced into car factories back in 1926, and while it made sense for manufacturing, it makes no sense for most other industries.

"There are so many industries that are project-based where you don't need eight hours, and just having someone keep themselves busy for eight hours, you're losing so much productivity," she said.

Her other point? The work week was designed for men who mostly had wives at home and who had relatively short commutes to work. Now, almost 100 years later, our workforce looks entirely different, and those rules that everyone has accepted as standard—well, they're simply outdated and make no sense.

Of course, many forward-thinking companies have been acknowledging this for years, but it took the pandemic for some businesses to start experimenting with doing things a different way. I can only hope that when the world completely goes back to "normal," these companies don't go backward too.

RULE #13: MOVE WITH THE TIMES

I'd like to think our business has stood the test of time for a couple of reasons. Perhaps the one I'm most proud of is that lots of our people have been with us for a long time. Amber was my first ever employee, and she's still with us sixteen years later. Our CEO, Olivia, has worked alongside me on and off for almost twenty years (she was with me in my previous company too). We also have a slew of leaders who are close to clocking up a decade with the organization, which I'm so grateful for.

Given that we've worked together for so long, we've really grown up together. We've been by each other's sides at our weddings. Amber was my bridesmaid, and my daughters were her flower girls. I was proud to be the emcee at Bec's wedding, and I traveled to Bali for Liv's wedding. We've consoled each other through break-ups and celebrated with each other when the right partners came along. We've comforted one another through miscarriages, cheered whenever one of us fell pregnant and supported each other through our childrens' births.

When we first started the business, I was in my mid-twenties, as were a lot of my team members. We hadn't yet started our own families, and life was a lot less complicated. As my babies came along, I started to study and think deeply about what I wanted the experience to be for my colleagues as they also entered this life phase. Through my own experience of having to figure out how I was going to continue to get my needs met and also now meet the needs of a baby, I was acutely aware of how hard it was. Had I not been my own boss, I could easily have dropped off the career ladder and chosen a different path. I didn't want that for me, and I didn't want it for my people. I had so much to give, and I felt the tug of having to be a role model to my children as much as I so dearly wanted to be a role model for my people.

I started to experiment with leaving the office early and with different forms of childcare, and as I experimented with this flexibility, it became clear to me that the number one priority for us to be able to retain our amazing people and also continue to grow our business was to create a flexible environment. And as time went on, I started to see how flexibility was needed not just for the parents in our organization but for the non-parents too.

I cache all of these learnings with a deep understanding of how privileged we are to even be having these conversations and how much privilege has played a part in our success. I also want to say how committed I am to using that privilege to make life better for others who haven't been given it.

When it comes to the businesses I've been privileged to start and build, I've always tried to hire great people and then trust them to do their jobs. Giving flexibility is one way of expressing gratitude to our people, but it's also a nod to the fact that the way we work has changed. Our ability to work in open-plan offices where it can be hard to focus for long periods of time has diminished. If you once commuted for hours a day to an office, you've likely just earned those hours back. The pandemic, while teaching us a ton of other valuable lessons, has shown us this for sure.

Flexibility means different things for me and my people. And as I said, it's not just the parents who need flexibility. We have a lot of people in the team who need more than just clocking in and clocking your needs at certain times.

My general manager, Amber, is from New Zealand. When we first met, she was living in Sydney and we worked together there in our office (which translated to a tiny little room at the front of my tiny little apartment). After many years of being in Australia, she started to feel the pull back to New Zealand, especially as she and her husband started trying for kids themselves. She wanted to be closer to her sisters and brother and the nieces and nephews that were coming along in fast succession.

Amber moved back home, and there were a few years there where she worked with a local company in Auckland. I missed her immensely during that time and asked her to come back into the business. I knew a big move wasn't in the cards, so if I wanted her back on the team, then we'd all just have to find a way to make it work. She initially started working on a schedule of three weeks in Auckland and then a week in the Sydney office, with a bit of leeway on either side if there was a major event on, or if there was no pressing need to be in either place. When Amber had her first baby we flexed again, having her drop down to part-time when her maternity leave ended and cutting out a lot of the travel until she was ready to ease herself back in.

When my chief of staff, Lucy, worked in Australia, she commuted each week from Melbourne up to our Sydney head-quarters. Until circumstances changed globally, she divided her time between Los Angeles and Melbourne and Sydney and went wherever the business (and I!) needed her most. This meant she often faced intense periods of work when she was in LA or Sydney when it was needed, but she then pulled back when she was home with her family in Melbourne. This nomadic way of living and working is not for everyone (and given the different time zones, it often meant Lucy started early and finished really late, and worked through weekends and over public holidays), but if you're looking for flexibility, excitement and autonomy, then this is the gig for you.

The rest of the team have full flexibility too. When the pandemic hit, our flexibility was taken to the next level, and it's stayed that way since. Our people now choose if they want to come into the office, and that generally means they feel more in control of their time and their work. Mostly, with the exception of a few company-wide meetings, they choose what hours they work as well.

When it comes to flexibility in the workplace more generally, I regularly see one of two things happening. I see companies insist on policing their employees' time, when people are really crying out to manage their own time so they can blend their two worlds of work and play. The other thing I see is companies that like to think they have a flexible culture when in reality their practices are far from that.

A business might have a written paternity leave policy but make jokes about any man who actually takes it. They might say they support working mothers yet roll their eyes at the mother who has to log off twenty minutes early to pick up her kid from daycare. They may say that flexibility extends to non-parents, too, but then there's an expectation that if overtime needs to happen, it's the twenty-somethings or the single people who should do that work. It feels to me that we're still operating in a structure that was built for our parents' generation, and if we want to build the best teams, attract the best talent and love the work we do, that's going to have to change. The structure needs to move with the times, and our leaders need to flex too.

I truly believe that the companies that don't respond to how their employees want to work and that don't do things differently are going to be left behind by other employers who are happy to be more progressive. Being generous with flexibility can be really hard work for employers. It certainly has been for us, but I've always been adamant that if we don't lead the way on it, then nothing will change.

RULE #14: NORMALIZE PREGNANCY

In April 2021, luggage and travel company AWAY appointed Jen Rubio as its new CEO. Ordinarily, this story wouldn't have much significance. After all, Jen was a co-founder of the business and had been acting as CEO for two months, which made her the obvious choice. But the fact that Jen was eight months pregnant at the time of her appointment makes the story a little more interesting.

"It's not lost on me that our board and investors, who have nearly $200 million invested in this company, encouraged me to take on the CEO role at eight months pregnant. I know this kind of support is not common in many companies—we need to change that," Jen wrote in an Instagram post.

Despite laws against pregnancy discrimination, in the past 10 years, there have been almost 50,000 claims filed in the United States. This is an extraordinarily high statistic that needs to be spoken about more and addressed in our workplaces. If you're an employer, it's important that you understand what constitutes discrimination, and if you're an employee, it's important to document every conversation and every interaction if you feel there's a chance you might be discriminated against.

I can vividly remember so many occasions of various team members over the years sharing their pregnancy news with me. I can tell you exactly where I was when they told me, and I can remember exactly how they told me. Each time I've jumped up and down in excitement with them, and on the few occasions people have felt worried about how they were going to manage and what the future might hold, I've sat them down and made a plan, promising them that we're in this together and we'll make it work. And somehow it has.

RULE #15: THE UNWRITTEN RULE

Back in 2014, Joe Biden—then vice president of the United States—sent a note to his team around the time of Thanksgiving. He wrote:

To My Wonderful Staff,

I would like to take a moment and make something clear to everyone. I do not expect nor do I want any of you to miss or sacrifice important family obligations for work.

Family obligations include but are not limited to family birthdays, anniversaries, weddings, any religious ceremonies such as first communions and bar mitzvahs, graduations, and times of need such as illness or a loss in the family.

This is very important to me. In fact, I will go so far as to say that if I find out that you are working with me while missing important family responsibilities, it will disappoint me greatly. This has been an unwritten rule since my days in the Senate.

Thank you all for the hard work.

The note was recirculated in the media around the time of his election to president, and I love it because it sends a clear message about the culture he wants to create in his team. It gives permission for his employees to bring their whole selves to work and prioritize their family obligations, setting the scene for what's acceptable and what's not.

I'd be willing to put money on the fact that any leader who adopts a similar philosophy will most likely get the best from their people just as soon as that first communion or bar mitzvah is over.

RULE #16: WHOSE KID IS THAT?

Last year I was working away at my desk and was super focused on a phone conversation. I had my head down and eyes closed, concentrating hard on whatever it was I was talking about, and wasn't aware of what was going on around me. When the call was over and I'd put down my phone, I looked to my right, and there was a little girl quietly sitting there who looked about three years old. She didn't belong to me (surprisingly), and I was pretty sure she didn't belong to any of my team members either. "Oh, hello!" I said. "Who are you?" Our creative director, Cecilia, jumped in and said that the toddler was her best friend's daughter. She explained that her friend had to go to an appointment with her husband and needed someone to watch her little girl for a few hours.

I freaking love that Cecilia knew this would not be a problem at all in our office. I love that no one on the team batted an eyelid and that everyone played their part to make that little girl feel welcome. What I love the most about this is that Cecilia knew we wouldn't mind her friend's daughter being dropped off one bit and didn't even think to ask—her friend was in need, and she did what she needed to do. Plus, Cecilia is a grown-up and knows that she can catch up on any work she needs to get done whenever she pleases. Turns out she didn't need to play catch-up because that kid was so well behaved and just colored the whole time anyway. (And on that note, where do I find one of those types of kids? Asking for a friend, of course . . .)

RULE #17: LET THEM CHOOSE

While working from home is an incredible experience for some people fortunate enough to have the room and the resources to design a space they love, for others it's tough. For people living with roommates, carving out a quiet space to work can be hard. For people with children at home, this also delivers a unique challenge (and I'm on good authority with this one—our schools were closed here in Los Angeles for thirteen months, and I had five kiddos virtual schooling at home). Not only did we parents have to work hard to keep the kids away from our work calls and meetings, we were passed another full-time job of ensuring they did their schoolwork. At one point, I calculated that I needed to be across 37 different software platforms in total, all of which required passwords and logins, just for the children to do their work. I struggle to remember my Apple ID on a good day, so this bit was hard for me.

As we found our stride and adjusted to the new way of working during the pandemic, I could see that my team, and many members of our community, were relishing the freedom that comes with remote work. For the vast majority of them, to be given the chance to skip the commute and stay at home in their UGG boots and pajama pants, only having to think about what to wear on top each day, was a wild, readily embraced concept.

But while the introverts among us thrived in the "virtual-first" model, there were also people on my team who I could see were not loving this new-found freedom as much. Sure, they liked their PJs for maybe one or two days a week, but they also missed talking about the latest *Survivor* episode with their co-workers and having a physical space to go to when they wanted to escape from home for a bit. Generally we're finding that most people who live near our headquarters will come into the office on a Tuesday because that's the day we have our all-hands weekly meeting. Some will come in every day. Some will choose to come in a handful of days per week. Some who moved interstate during the pandemic simply dial in. It's their choice.

RULE #18: LEAVE LOUDLY

I need to leave work early to see my therapist about my anxiety over leaving work early.

Unknown

Women and men—listen up! I want you to start being proud of when you're leaving the office or finishing up for the day to go do whatever it is that you need to do next—be it picking up a kid from school, going to visit an elderly parent, or going to the gym. Be proud that you've given your all and now you deserve the opportunity to do the other stuff that matters to you too. And please, please, I beg of you: don't skulk out silently feeling guilty, leaving everyone wondering where you've gone. No one wins from such martyrdom. Stand up, be proud, and for goodness sake, leave loudly.

RULE #19: FLEXIBILITY WORKS BOTH WAYS

What we've learned over the years is that we do need to have some rules and that we also need flexibility on the side of the employee. It must work both ways. If I'm going to create a culture where people don't lie about going to the hairdresser or going to see their accountant on a Thursday afternoon; or they work from home when they want; or they leave early for a school pickup, that doesn't come without some compromise. There are of course the occasional times when I expect people to answer an email at night or on a Saturday if it's really urgent. It's when your employer is expecting you to write back to that weekend email every single time and be in the office ten hours a day that you have a problem.

For the most part, flexibility in my company works because my team members are grown-ups and they're able to self-regulate, and I've found that when I'm flexible with them, they're happy with me. When they're happy, they're happy to work hard. We all win.

enjoy.

In the same way we've trained ourselves to default to "I'm so busy," we're also conditioned to default to "Gahhh, I've got to go to work" like it's the worst thing in the world. What if we were to bring an awareness to this and change our language and thinking around our work? What if we started to think about our work more as a form of self-expression, almost art if you will—your chance to create something cool, to give others some enjoyment, to change someone's day? You might not be able to do that with the technical part of your work, but I can guarantee you that you have it within your power to make the ride more fun for your co-workers, more memorable for your customers and more fulfilling for yourself if you just change the lens (and the language) a little. I get that the day-to-day grind can be challenging, but the new hustle wants you to think less about the ten "urgent" emails in your inbox and more about the people you work with, the values you all hold true and how you can play a part in making work fun.

RULE #20: THE DINNER PARTY TEST

There's a way to tell if your culture is working and if employees are proud to be part of your business. I call it the dinner party test. Imagine this. A Disneyland team member (ahem, a "cast member") is at a dinner party one Saturday night and gets asked the question: "So what do you do?" Walt Disney would likely turn in his grave if he overheard the team member say, "Oh, I'm a ride operator at a theme park." To pass the dinner party test, what we need to hear is "I work at Disneyland." People who are proud of where they work mention this first. What they do is secondary to the pride they feel by stepping through your doors every day.

RULE #21: GET OUT THE POST-IT NOTES

Today you are You, that is truer than true.
There is no one alive who is Youer than You.

Dr. Seuss

We agonized about getting our core values right for years. We'd table them at every strategic planning day and debate them for hours on end. Mostly these debates failed, and we'd finish the strategy day without a set of core values we could unanimously agree upon. I'd always encourage the team by saying, "Let's be patient. These things take time, and they have to feel right to us. Let's not push it."

Volume was never the problem. We were always able to throw a ton of colorful Post-it Notes up on a wall, but the hard part was whittling them down to a group of values that felt exactly like us. As well as being succinct, the other hard part was having the courage to make them so distinctive that all team members—existing and future—would never mistake them as belonging to someone else. Aggressive authenticity is what's required when designing core values, because they're the cornerstone of your company's culture.

Your core values go a long way in showing the world who you are and why someone should work with you, either as a team member or a client. Core values form the basis for how things are done differently in your business and provide a beautiful guide for your people as to how you want them to behave. Contrary to what you might think, core values shouldn't be like arriving home after a long day and putting on a cozy, soft sweater. If they're comfortable, you're working to the wrong set of values. It takes effort and discipline to stand up for what you believe in rather than bend to a more accepted, mainstream way of thinking.

Here are some sets of core values from companies I admire:

Atlassian Open company, no bullshit. Build with heart and balance. Don't f%&! the customer. Play as a team. Be the change you seek.

Boston Consulting Group Digital Ventures Redefine your limits. Don't fear fear. Impact over words. Seek difference. Build partnerships.

Zappos Deliver WOW through service. Create fun and a little weirdness. Be adventurous, creative and open-minded. Be humble.

So many businesses get their core values wrong. They make them so generic that they could belong to any company on the planet—"customer service," "teamwork," and "success"—and then wonder why no one's really into them. However, when I read the preceding ones, I really get a sense of what these companies stand for, and it makes me want to know more.

In the early days of a company's life, core values are less necessary because you'll see them embodied in its founders: the way they act, the way they think, what they value and what they don't. Over time, as a company scales and the founder is less available to everyone, it's important that these qualities and behaviors get extracted from the founder's brain and implanted into the company playbook. Write 'em down, but more importantly, live and breathe these babies. Every. Single. Day. Have them become part of your company folklore. Use them to tell stories. Use them to catalyze action. Use them to make decisions. Use them to hire and fire. Make them so unforgettable that they'll inspire your team each time they hear them.

I'm pleased to report that all those colorful Post-it Notes eventually worked a charm, and we nailed our core values. And yep, you'll notice that some of them I've included as rules in this book too. Here goes with ours:

Members first. Create memories and moments. Believe it's possible. Do the right work. Care the most. Jump in the pool. Above all, inspire.

RULE #22: JUMP IN THE POOL

I do take my work seriously. And the way to do that is to not take yourself too seriously.

Alan Rickman

Of all our core values, my favorite would have to be "jump in the pool," which might make no sense to you at all, but holds a lot of meaning for us. This value always brings us back to who we are as a business and who we strive to be as a bunch of humans navigating life together. It helps us sense-check if we're on the right path or if we've lost our way a little. Sometimes businesses, and the people who run them, get so caught up in solving the wrong problems and forget what's actually important. Getting back to our core values is an excellent way to reorientate everyone and remind ourselves why we do what we do.

I can't tell you exactly when jumping in the pool became an important metaphor for us. Perhaps it was on one of our first Leadership Gatherings on Necker Island where Sir Richard Branson threw me in the pool completely clothed after we'd finished the last session. Everyone else followed suit, jumping in one by one. Watching the group bob around in the water with smiles from ear to ear, music blaring, high-fiving each other is a sight I've seen a hundred times now during Business Chicks experiences. For me, jumping in the pool means not taking yourself too seriously, not worrying if your clothes get wet, not thinking about the way you look, not worrying what others think of you and letting go of the moment enough to just enjoy it. It's getting back to being a kid again and finding happiness in being silly, and when it comes down to it, it's all about creating a little bit of joy and making a memory for someone else.

For some of our members, jumping in the pool represents getting out of their comfort zone and shedding the armor that they have to wear each day when they go into their workplaces, pretending to be someone they're not. It's about forgetting the roles and responsibilities they carry each day, not just at work but in their personal lives, too. Or it's doing something they don't really want to do but know deep down that if they do it they'll be proud of themselves afterward. No one needs to literally get in a pool to do that, but for some it can be the catalyst to living a little more bravely.

Jumping in the pool or encouraging people to play more and get out of their comfort zone manifests for us as a business in other ways. Since before I can remember, I've loved dressing up and going to fancy dress parties. I know for some people this may seem like your perfect idea of hell, and just the thought of having to do this sends you straight into a cold sweat. What I've also experienced, though, over many years, is that dressing up is just another metaphor for getting out of your comfort zone and being silly, and it's something we've experimented with successfully a bunch of times.

A good friend of mine, Cathie Reid, agrees with this thinking, and it's underpinned the culture in her business, Icon Group, for many years now. Cathie and her husband, Stuart, started out in 1998 and have built the business into an extraordinary success story with a valuation of well over $1 billion.

"Since I can remember we've been holding all of our major internal strategy and management days in costume," Cathie says. "Twenty years ago it started with Stuart and me thinking of ways we could bring a bit of theater to the day on a very low budget, while at the same time providing a theme to link the overall goals of the company to. The biggest upside to this strategy was the change in attitude that turning up in costume brings. Days when you bring your entire leadership group together come at a significant investment, regardless of the actual cost of the venue and any guest presenters you may have contracted. You've taken all of your leaders away from their teams and their day jobs, and you really want everyone to bring a different attitude and mindset to the day. There's no faster way to make people feel different, and slightly uncomfortable, than by having them turn up in costume! No one thinks the same way when wearing a costume as they do when they're wearing their usual corporate uniform, whatever form that takes."

Cathie told me that over the past twenty years their dressing up has become an important part of the company's culture. She says that there's always a high degree of anticipation around what the theme of the day will be, and once it's announced, the race for the best costume begins. "We often see groups of managers from within regions or divisions team up to deliver an entire story—the finance division's presentation as the cast of *Game of Thrones* with part of the script delivered in Dothraki will never be forgotten!" For Cathie and Stuart's business (which now employs over 3,000 people across Australia,

Singapore, New Zealand, China, Vietnam and Hong Kong), the process has become highly competitive and a part of their company culture that's non-negotiable to keep alive.

Cathie and Stuart would never miss a step, but there have been times when, as a business, we've gotten it wrong and forgotten to metaphorically jump in the pool. At one of our annual conferences, we decided that the theme for the final night party should be "A Touch of Gold," which, looking back, was really not us at all. This theme got no one out of their comfort zones, and that night no one jumped in the pool. We all looked pretty and well put together in our sparkly dresses and gold accessories, yes, but nothing moved us to be anyone different from who we already thought we needed to be in our everyday lives. It was a departure from the previous year's conference where everyone had dressed up in fancy dress and hardly even stopped to eat their meal as they were having too much fun on the dance floor.

Do you think the times we got it right will go down as some of the most joyful occasions we've ever experienced? Do you think we'll remember them for years to come? Do you think they're a source of happy memories we can access whenever we need? They sure are. Whenever things go awry, or we forget who we want to be as humans inspiring other humans to be all they can be, we always find ourselves a pool to jump into, fancy dress and all.

RULE #23: FIND THE GAYLE TO YOUR OPRAH

My mother worked as a teacher at the same school for twenty-four years. She adored her job and got so much from it, but in the end, the thing that kept her there more than anything else was her friendships. She is now retired, which was a decision she agonized over for the final few years because she couldn't bear the thought of not seeing her "work wife" each day.

If you've got "your person" at work, just as my mom had, chances are you're doing okay on the work and happiness front. And that's scientifically proven, too. According to a Gallup poll, people who have a best friend at work are seven times (yes, seven times) more likely "to be engaged in their jobs, are better at relating to customers, produce higher-quality work and have greater well-being."

The *Washington Post* recently ran an article saying that for many of us, the pandemic was made even harder by not having that person around all the time. In an already stressful and hyper-anxious time, not being able to laugh at a joke and work alongside those who remembered the way we like our coffee only added another layer of disappointment. It also encouraged workplaces to consider this unique dynamic of relationships as they decided to either re-open their physical office spaces or keep their workforces completely remote.

Having a work wife also means we're more invested in our companies because we're so invested in this particular relationship. Having someone you can vent to and someone who can finish your sentences makes the day not only fly by but also makes work something you genuinely cherish.

A work wife is someone who laughs along with you (or at you!). They're there when you need an email edited or some advice on how to tackle a certain situation. They're invested in your success and want to see you do well, in the exact same way you want to see them nail their next presentation or get the pay raise they deserve.

If you're lucky enough to already enjoy the benefits of a friendship with your work wife, be sure to tell them how much they mean to you. And if you don't yet have a Gayle to your Oprah? An Amy to your Tina? A Thelma to your Louise? Either go hunt one down intentionally or ask yourself if you're in the right job or right company.

RULE #24: GREET EVERYONE, EVERY TIME

When you walk into the office and head straight to your desk, it sends a subconscious message that you're only there for you and your work. When you walk in and greet your teammates, it sends a message that you're a team, and you're in this together.

Same goes when you jump on a Zoom call. Don't just arrive at the meeting and look away from your screen or, worse, keep typing or being busy and distracted elsewhere. Be there, be present, be friendly.

Get known as the person who cares about everyone and makes a point of greeting all team members. You don't need to bounce in like an excitable toddler on a trampoline, but a warm and upbeat "Good morning!" or "How are you?" will always be appreciated.

For the introverts out there, I understand this might be difficult to try. Even just a little awkward wave and smile can go a long way.

RULE #25: NO DAYS OFF FOR YOUR BIRTHDAY

Ever worked in a business where you can tell they're trying to get it right, but their efforts don't really stack up? They try to force culture by systemizing staff drinks when it was already working with you just having an occasional catch-up with your teammates whenever you wanted to? Suddenly the impromptu Friday afternoon drink you were looking forward to with a few of your colleagues makes it feel like you now have to stay back and socialize with management, too. It suddenly becomes a "work thing" you must do.

Sometimes culture loses impact when we over-engineer it. I'm all for getting the team together to go bowling or maybe have a scavenger hunt around the city, but there's also a lot to be said for letting it unfold organically. This is a lot easier when you have clever senior leaders who emphasize culture as a business priority and understand that culture is much more than supplying free tampons in the women's bathrooms or making sure the cereal is stocked in the kitchen.

When we over-engineer culture, we also make assumptions that might not necessarily be true. For example, I've always loved going into the office on my birthday. My team have always celebrated me because I've always done my best to celebrate them. There's always a card and maybe a balloon and a cake. There's always cake.

A dear friend of mine, Natasha, told me that in her company, they recently instigated a new rule that you're not allowed to come into work on your birthday. They thought they were being really generous and were working on the assumption that everybody would like to have the day off for their birthday. The problem is, Natasha is single and lives alone and also happens to love her work. And besides, everyone she'd want to hang out with (her friends, her mom!) would be working that day anyway, and she didn't want to have to ask them to also take a day off. Natasha leads a small team of seven people and genuinely enjoys their company. She likes the everyday banter and the jokes that make the hours fly by most days. She told me that, for her small team, the new company-wide rule really disappointed her and her colleagues. "We had a little thing going on where we'd put up signs at our colleagues' desks for their birthday every year and decorate their chairs and always sing them happy birthday and give them a gift. It was just a little thing, but we'd been doing it for my whole team for the six years I've been there, and everyone loved those days. It was something we looked forward to." She raised it with the powers that be in her firm, and they told her she had to play ball and make her team not come in on their birthday so it would be "fair for everyone" and so the rule could be adhered to across the board.

By all means give your people a day off in celebration of their birthday—but let them take that day at any time. If they want to celebrate with their friends at work and wear a birthday party hat all day and be showered in a little desk confetti, then let them!

RULE #26: EAT THE CARROT CAKE

Birthdays are great opportunities to celebrate and make our workplaces a little happier, if only for a moment. In our business, when team members first start with us we ask what their favorite type of cake is. When their birthday rolls around, of course that's what they get. It's funny how people still seem a little surprised by this. "Yum, carrot cake—that's my fave!" Um, yeah, we know. We also give them a gift and make everyone sing loudly and poorly (wait, maybe that's just me), and it's not uncommon for someone to walk in on their birthday to a desk covered in streamers and balloons, just like the way it used to be in Natasha's company. We've also developed a tradition where team members have to wear a fluorescent pink cape for the day . . . and yes, they wear it to meetings and when they go to lunch, too.

I told the birthday cape story to a friend recently, and she asked, "But what if a client is coming into the office that day?" It was easy to answer her. If a client doesn't appreciate that we're the kind of business that wants to have fun, they're probably not the right client for us.

Anniversaries should also be celebrated, as should big wins and career highlights. There's a Los Angeles start-up called SnackNation that is in the business of distributing snacks into corporate offices across America. We got to visit their head-quarters, and one of the first things I noticed was the giant helium balloons behind their chairs. These balloons were in the shape of numbers, and when we quizzed their head of people and culture about them, she explained that they were anniversary balloons to celebrate the number of years a team member had worked there. At SnackNation, they focus on celebrating achievements and behaviors above everything else. They say that emotions and performance are directly linked and that by celebrating anniversaries, you'll engage people in a way that will likely be emotional for them.

We send flowers to our employees on their anniversaries, and we also stop to celebrate when a team member signs a big deal or when we achieve some other milestone.

When my first book *Winging It* was released, my team celebrated by throwing me a surprise party in our headquarters. They deliberately timed a media interview the day before the release of the book and set me up in a small room for the hour-long chat. While I was being interviewed, they went into overdrive, completely transforming the office outside into a sea of balloons, confetti, my favorite people, music and cocktails. My whole team was there, my family and kids were there, my publisher was there, and once I got over the initial shock of what was happening, I also noticed that my best friend and her husband had flown in for the occasion as well!

In the midst of the madness of a book release, those first few hectic days could have easily passed by without a lot of celebration and just a ton of nose-to-the-grindstone effort, but the team took the time to mark the occasion, and it was exactly what I needed to stop and appreciate the moment too. I'll never forget it as long as I live.

begin.

I'm often asked by young people how they can get the best possible start in their careers and set themselves up for the best chance at success. Yes, it's important to make yourself indispensable, to go above and beyond, to not just do your job—all these things matter—but there are other ideas worth considering here too.

There's sometimes friction between us oldies who have had to fight and earn every reward we've achieved and the millennials who are often seen as presumptuous and expecting far too much far too soon. I'm not going to weigh into that debate as I believe millennials can bring so much to the table, but I also believe in tapping into the wisdom of people who've built amazing careers and navigated a ton of problems that millennials will eventually have to solve too.

If that's you, I offer these few anecdotes that I hope you'll take to heart and use as you forge your own way on your own terms. Even if you're not a spring chicken starting out, perhaps you'll find some of these insights useful too . . .

RULE #27: YOU DON'T NEED A MENTOR

I've been really lucky to have a diverse group of mentors throughout my career. There was the rich, semi-retired dude who made me cry every time I left a session with him. That one was fun. I was always on the brink of making up an excuse as to why I couldn't make a session, and while I hated every minute of my time with him, I ultimately learned so much. He constantly dismissed me and made me feel so small, and this only spurred me to want to do better and prove him wrong. He'd say things to me like "There's no real money to be made in that women's thing you do" and "I think you should consider looking at another business instead of this one" when I knew in my heart I was on the right track. Another one of my mentors was a firm but caring woman who was forty years older than me. She was always tough and never let me off the hook, but at the same time was able to encourage me along and drill into me the importance of things like discipline, productivity and managing my time.

I've had several other mentoring relationships as well, and what I've learned along the way is that it's impossible to have all your needs met by one mentor. The experience you need and the questions you want answered can't be found in just one person. They'd be a miracle worker if so.

Think of this concept as if you're a professional athlete. Your massage therapist who keeps you supple is different from your physiotherapist who helps with strength and injuries, who's different from your mindset coach who gets you championship-ready, who's different from your manager who does all those amazing ambassadorship deals and fights off all the teams who want you, who's different from your coach who keeps you fit and on track.

As I've grown as a leader and business owner, I've adopted this athlete idea and approached different mentors for different problems. There are my mentors who I contact when I have a question about money, tax, finances, the stock market and investing, and so on. I have mentors who I turn to whenever I have a question about people problems I'm facing. I even have a couple of mentors who I'd consider spiritual advisors and who I can pick up the phone to if I'm grappling with some thoughts that need higher placement. You might benefit from sitting down and writing a small list of the areas in your life that you could do with some guidance in, and then listing the people you know—or you'd like to know—who could help with them. Building a circle of trusted advisors is the new hustle's version of having a single mentor, and this crew bring an array of skills and ideas and points of views. Call 'em your dream team.

I want to give you a little piece of advice here now too if you'll take it: never ask someone to be your mentor. I'm saying this from the point of view of a person who gets asked this question quite a lot. Whenever I get asked to be someone's mentor, I want to run for the hills. Yes, I mentor quite a few people, and yes, I enjoy it immensely, but when you ask me, "Will you be my mentor?" you're asking me to commit to a relationship I can't always carve out time for.

The much more palatable alternative is to be strategic and succinct. You might say, "I admire you a lot and am needing a boost in my career or business. Would it be okay if I emailed you two questions that I need help with, and then can we schedule a quick fifteen-minute phone catch-up to go through those two questions?" My answer would likely be a "hell, yes" I want to be able to help others, but you need to make it easy. By sending the questions in advance, you give your potential mentor time to think through how they can best serve you and not be put on the spot. You're also showing a deep respect for their time. If the person agrees to your phone call, make sure you keep it to the timeframe you promised.

Simplifying the ask will go a long way to building your dream team of mentors who'll help you win every step of the way.

RULE #28: SIT IN THEIR SEAT

A friend of mine, Dana, works as the head of marketing for a solar company. They install solar panels on homes across America, and she tells me that her work makes her feel good. It makes her feel as though she's contributing in a small way to cooling the planet and making a difference. Her entire team feel this way too. For her, the purpose of the company—to be a part of the climate change solution—is a given, and not what she's looking for when she hires for her team. You see, for Dana, if you're going to apply to their company and do the sort of work they're doing, it's an absolute assumption that you're going to care about the environment. The fact that you care about the environment, however, doesn't solve Dana's everyday problems, such as how she's going to attract more customers, communicate more effectively, be better than her competitors and so the list goes on.

Same goes for our work at Business Chicks. We're also a mission-led company—we make the world a better place for women—but I can't tell you how many times over the years people have gotten their approach wrong when applying for a role with us. They've spent their entire cover letter preaching about how much they want to change the status quo for women and how if they're given the opportunity, they'll make sure this happens. Being this idealistic is inspiring and necessary, but just like for Dana, these ideals alone won't solve our business problems.

When you're applying for a role or pitching to a new client for their business, get clear on this one and put yourself in their shoes for a minute. You're there to solve their problems and not just agree with their philosophies. What this means is that a job applicant should first try to understand the frustrations and challenges of Dana's role and then tell her how they're going to fix them. I'd spend all of my time doing that first and maybe add in a PS like this at the end to seal the deal:

PS It goes without saying that I'm relentlessly passionate about climate change and putting good work out into the world so we can turn this climate thing around. In college, I ran the climate science club; I've traveled the world attending climate summits; I compost, drive an electric car, recycle everything and I've also been a volunteer for the past five years cleaning up our beaches.

I can't tell you the number of job applications that I've read or the interviews I've sat through where the only focus from the applicant is our mission. Like Dana, this is a baseline assumption for me.

Try to understand what might cause potential employers or clients stress, where a new opportunity might lie, what their challenges are. Once you've zeroed in on these areas, you're only then ready to convince them that you're the right person for the job and that the planet matters and so do women.

RULE #29: DON'T EXPECT A PROMOTION JUST FOR SHOWING UP

Over the years I've had a number of people come to me saying they need a pay raise because they want to go on a holiday or move into a bigger condo. Um, that's great, and I love your ambition, but as a manager, those reasons are not problems for me to solve for you.

All strong managers want their people to succeed, but when it comes to dishing out rewards and incentives, they need to know what you did above and beyond your role. How did you make an impact that no one else did? How did you add value?

I've never once said no to a pay raise where the argument is built on fact and I can see the extra value that person has brought to the business and our bottom line.

If you're looking for a pay increase or a little extra responsibility, here are a few tips worth considering.

Time it right Remember that December and January are typically slow months for most businesses and generally not the time to be asking for more money.

Start positive and never threaten Open the conversation with all the positive things you love about your role and the company and don't threaten to leave the business if you don't get your own way. You'll only come across as a toddler about to have a meltdown if you don't get the toy you feel you deserve. These situations require all your emotional faculties to be in order and for you to appear calm and collected the whole time.

Never let it be a surprise Take the time to approach your manager a week or so before and let them know what you want to discuss so they can at least start to think about a solution too. And do your homework. Come to the chat prepared with examples—have your points written down in case you forget them and be ready to address each one individually.

Demonstrate why It surprises me that people often forget that leaders are running budgets and need to know how giving you more money will yield better business outcomes for the company. Work hard to demonstrate your plans for how you're going to at least make back the pay increase you're asking for, and try to get your manager inspired about what this will mean for them and the results you're going to achieve.

Know your number Don't offer a couple of options of what you're looking for, just offer one. We once had an employee ask one of our leaders for a pay raise of "between $2,000 and $10,000." You can probably see how that range didn't work in that person's favor.

Talk, then shut up As with every solid negotiation, state your case and your number, and then be quiet. Resist the urge to talk. The first person to speak after that number is out of your mouth generally loses the negotiation. Language matters here too. If you say, "I was hoping for $5,000 more," it weakens your ask. Say: "I'm asking for $5,000." It's a tiny nuance, but it makes the ask stronger.

RULE #30: OWN YOUR MISTAKES

We've made a ton of mistakes over the years. Some of them have been inconsequential enough, and others have sent us hiding under the desk for a few moments to recover.

There was the time one of our junior staffers accidentally emailed our entire database, and the message began with "Dear First Name" instead of including the recipients' actual first names. Eek. As soon as she realized what she'd done, she didn't hide or back away at all, immediately bringing the mistake to her manager and popping a note in the company's group chat explaining how she'd made that slip-up.

Compare this accountability with the behavior of people who won't admit they're blatantly responsible, instead giving long-winded stories about what happened and apportioning blame to ten different other contributing factors.

There's nothing more frustrating for me than hearing about a mistake that's been made in my business, and no one has owned up to it. I care less about the mistake and more about the honesty and integrity that goes with the admission. You'll get so much further ahead in your career and life if you can say, "Dang, that was me! I'm so sorry!" rather than avoiding admitting the mistake and hiding in the shadows of your own fear.

And the most important point of all this? You can screw up all you like—just don't make the exact same mistake twice.

RULE #31: SAY YES

Find a way to say yes to things. Say yes to invitations to a
new country, say yes to meet new friends, say yes
to learn something new. Yes is how you get your first job,
and your next job, and your spouse, and even your kids.

Eric Schmidt, former CEO

and chairman of Google

Okay, okay, I totally understand that in theory, this rule completely contradicts my earlier rule, "Learn how to say no," but I'm assuming you'll work out the difference here. Learning how to say no effectively is all about boundary setting and understanding how to turn down the things that aren't going to move your game forward. What I'm asking of you here with *this* rule is to say yes to the stuff that is going to move you forward.

One of my favorite stories of saying yes comes from television producer and screenwriter Shonda Rhimes, who is the brains behind shows like *Scandal, Grey's Anatomy* and *How to Get Away with Murder*. One Thanksgiving, Shonda was having dinner with her sister Delores and telling her about some of the invitations she was receiving as her profile continued to grow in the industry. Speaking engagements, Hollywood parties . . . you name the opportunity, Shonda was being offered it. But her sister remained indifferent to Shonda's musings.

"Who cares?" Delores said. "You never say yes to anything anyway."

It was that moment, hearing that comment from her sister, that made Shonda realize that despite her success, she was hiding from life and was miserable as a result. So in her sister's dining room that night, Shonda vowed to say yes to unexpected invitations and opportunities.

For one year, she said yes to anything that made her nervous and anything that forced her out of her comfort zone—speaking in public, going on live television, meeting with the president of the United States, losing 100 pounds. In doing so, she changed her life. "The very act of doing the thing that scared me undid the fear and made it not scary," she said in a TED Talk aptly named "My Year of Saying Yes to Everything."

Saying yes might not mean meeting with a president, or anything near as intimidating. Saying yes when you don't have all the answers might be as simple as putting your hand up when your boss asks for a volunteer, or having that conversation about a new job even though you're happy where you are. Opportunities often arise from unexpected places—that serendipitous chat with someone in the elevator, a chance meeting at the barbecue you weren't going to go to, or attending a business conference with a bunch of people you don't know. Starting by saying yes regularly to smaller situations may just be the door-opener you need to reach bigger horizons.

What I love about Shonda's story of saying yes is that she didn't start with the intention of creating a TED Talk or writing a book. She said yes because she knew it was what she needed to do. When a publisher approached her about turning the year into a book, she said yes. After everything she had just created for herself, how could she not?

RULE #32: STOP LOOKING FOR YOUR PASSION

I reckon far too many people get caught up in trying to find their passion and searching for their purpose. There's nothing to be found. It's not there. It doesn't exist. Stop looking.

I believe you can't find your passion without stumbling into it. The secret is that it's found by accident. It's discovered by honing what you love and whittling away at what you don't— but guess what? None of that can happen without a decent amount of doing, not thinking. No amount of thinking about your passion and purpose will make it actualize.

I'm passionate about a million things, such as helping others, working alongside clever people, helping women gain more power, making money, being kind, uncovering talent, amplifying the voices of underprivileged people, coaching smart people, learning and so the list goes on. But if I'd been looking for a job with all those things twenty years ago, there's no way I would have found it. It would have been an impossible task.

Instead of running around and trying to find your passion, just do the things that light you up. Do the things that come naturally to you. Do the things that you find easy, effortless even. Do more of the things that make time go by quickly, and do the things that you're good at.

It's not new thinking, but it works: stop wasting time trying to get it right. Just start somewhere and keep going. Eventually, all will be revealed.

relate.

An old friend of mine had a beautiful relationship with her elderly grandparents, who were the most tender and loving couple. I looked up to them and admired the way they lived so effortlessly together, having such different interests yet enjoying each other's company at the same time. She would putter in the garden alone for hours on end and walk the dog without fail every morning and night, staying up late to watch her favorite television programs. He was happier down at the beach in the water and whiling away the rest of the day reading a book and getting into bed early each night. In their eighties, it made more sense for them to sleep in different beds where they'd have the best chance at a good night's sleep, and yet they'd also make an effort to find moments in the day to spend time together and connect over their meals and cups of tea.

My friend and I would often get out of the city and go and stay with them for the weekend. Their energy was so gentle and reminded us about what mattered most and what was really important.

We watched as her grandfather fell ill with cancer and started to lose weight dramatically. He seemed to get so frail so quickly. Her grandmother was stoic throughout this time, tending to him around the clock and doing what she could to both make this time as gentle as possible but also come to terms with the fact that the end had come sooner than either of them had thought it would.

Toward the final few weeks of his life, the grandfather asked to speak with me alone. I sat on the side of his bed as he asked if I'd help him with a secret job. He made me promise that I wouldn't tell anyone about it until he was gone. He directed me to some money he'd been hiding and told me there was a bracelet he wanted to buy for his wife. He asked me to take the money and go down to their local jeweler to buy it for her. Unable to walk now, this was obviously a plan the grandfather had been scheming for some time as the jeweler knew the exact piece I'd been sent to collect.

The grandfather was so frail at this point that he couldn't find the strength to write in the card I'd bought to accompany the gift. He knew exactly what he wanted to say and had me write these words: "Not for any reason, but for every reason."

I'd never seen the grandmother cry once during those last few months of his life, but when I handed over the jewelery box on the day of his funeral and she read the words in the card, she sobbed without control. His gesture seemed a perfect end to their full life together.

The sentiment behind his words has always stuck with me, and the memory of his kindness and thoughtfulness having such an impact on another person is something that I'll never forget.

We don't need a love story or a death to remind us to be kind to one another. We don't need any reason or excuse to make someone's day (or life). To be kind, to be thoughtful, to think of others, to care—these are all wonderful practices, and they're practices that shouldn't be reserved just for home, but for our workplaces too.

RULE #33: POINT THE FINGER

One of the small joys of my pandemic experience was locking myself in my home office and interviewing some extraordinarily clever people for our digital events. One of my favorite interviews was with US soccer champion and ex–professional athlete Abby Wambach. As well as being funny, down-to-earth and unassuming, Abby dished out some solid advice about building teams that perform.

During her career, Abby won two Olympic gold medals and scored 184 goals, which at her retirement made her the highest goal-scoring soccer player (male or female) of all time. In our conversation, she told me how she watched a replay of one of her old games with her wife, Glennon Doyle, and their kids. One of the kids, Amma, noticed that each time Abby scored a goal she'd start pointing at her teammates, and Amma wanted to know why.

Abby explained that those goals weren't about her; they were about the effort from all her teammates who had set her up to make that goal happen. By pointing at them and directing some praise their way, she was sharing the triumph and ensuring they knew how appreciated they were.

In my conversation with Abby, she said, "In every soccer game, there is hopefully a goal. And when a goal is scored, I can tell everything I want to know about that team. I can tell if their teammates like the goal scorer, I can tell if their teammates like the assist maker. I can tell if they respect their coaches or if the players respect the bench players. There is so much to be learned from watching and observing a team by the way they act when they win."

Good people know that one of the best ways to become liked and respected is to be overt with giving credit where credit's due. It's about calling out good work and making sure everyone else knows about it too. If you can build a reputation as someone who is always cheerleading for others, always "pointing the finger," you'll build your value as a positive and useful person to have around. This might mean dropping a note in your company's group chat, sending an email to the whole team or mentioning it in the team meeting. We do a form of finger-pointing in our business: each week in our company-wide meeting, we ask for the "win of the week" and shout out the colleague who's contributed in some special way. It feels good to be seen, and it feels good to give praise. Think about your colleagues and their work this past week—is there someone you can point the finger at? Go on then, you'll make their day.

RULE #34: ANOTHER GLASS OF WATER

A single act of kindness throws out roots in all directions, and the roots spring up and make new trees.

Amelia Earhart

You know what's a great way to get a co-worker to love you? Whenever you get a glass of water from the office kitchen for yourself, get two. Get one for you and one for someone else. Just plonk it right down and say, "There you go." Or . . . when you go fill up your water bottle, grab theirs and fill it up too. This idea sounds so obvious, but you'd be so surprised at the number of people who don't think this way and are only ever thinking of their own needs. If you're getting a cup of coffee for yourself, yell out, "I'm getting coffee! Who wants one?" You're doing the thing anyway, so do it for someone else too.

My kids are constantly asking, "Can I have water? Can I have some water? Can you get me a glass of water?" like thirty times minimum a day. When we were building our house, my ex-husband had the idea to install a mini water filter station near our kitchen. We always have cups sitting right by that water fountain, and the lever is at kid height so that even a three-year-old can reach and get her own water. I reckon we save approximately half an hour a day through this self-service stroke of genius.

Grown-ups use the station all the time too. The other day, while I was getting a glass for me, I saw that our babysitter had left her empty water bottle there. As with every person who helps care for kids, she'd obviously started to fill her bottle up, and another task had distracted her elsewhere. I took the water bottle, filled it up, and placed it back where I'd found it. It took me ten seconds, but when I heard her walking around the house going into every room and asking everybody "Was that you who did that for me?" I knew she'd appreciated the gesture.

RULE #35: WORTH DOING

Any chance you get to make someone's day, to stand out a little and to make a memory for someone else—these are things worth doing.

Sometimes my team think I'm nuts when, with only a few hours to go until our next event, I ask them to go down to the shops, buy twenty boxes of chocolates and bring them back to the office. They think I'm nuts when I sit there and hand-write twenty cards to go with those boxes of chocolates for the members I know will be at that event. Members who have supported us for years. Members who I know will appreciate the care we're showing by thanking them this way. To me, this activity is inconceivably precious and is worth doing.

Let's not get confused here about showing gratitude: it doesn't need to cost a lot of money. If you're intentional with your thanks and go to a bit of effort, then that act can be just as meaningful as a huge bunch of expensive flowers. Even a thoughtful email can go a long way—it's all in the delivery and the generosity of your message.

Here are some ways to say thank you that matter:

Power up the personalization After I interviewed Abby Wambach, I sent her a little figurine of a wolf to say thank you. She wrote the book *Wolfpack*, so I thought she might get a kick out of this. I also included a figurine of a small cheetah for her wife, Glennon. This would make sense to you if you've read her book *Untamed*, where the opening story is about a cheetah named Tabitha. I'm told both the wolf and cheetah were a hit in their house!

Give gifts I mean, no-brainer, right? Well no, you've still got to think this through. No point in sending a bottle of champagne to someone who doesn't drink, or a beautiful candle to someone who owns a homewares store and can get them at wholesale herself. A note here too: don't disguise your company merch (unless it's the best thing ever) as a gift. I've been sent some random stuff with logos on it in lieu of a gift— mousepad, anyone?

An email, a card, a letter, or even a book As I said, a thoughtful email can go a long way. Choose your words carefully, be generous with what you say, and be genuine and purposeful. A handwritten card is even better, of course, and a letter can also be a gorgeous way to say you're grateful. I've had two separate Business Chicks members now create a book for me (yes!) filled with memories and stories of how we've helped and inspired them. Receiving these is pretty freaking special, and you can make your own on any of those photobook sites.

Just between you and me... some of the best ways I've thanked others for a job well done is to turn a personal joke into something a little more special. When I published my last book, I fell in love with my editor Georgia. Just as the book was going to the printers, she let me know that this was my final chance to change anything. I wrote back and said, nope, you're good to go, all fine here; so she sent the file off to the printers. A couple of weeks later, I thought I'd play a prank on her, so I emailed saying, "Georgia, I found a typo on page 187!" She wrote back freaking out and saying it was too late. I let her suffer for a full ten minutes before I told her I was just kidding. Her response was "You can't do that to me! I had a heart attack. I'm just a cardigan-wearing editor!" When the book was eventually published, I bought her a quirky cardigan as a thank-you gift. The best part of this story? The next time I surprised her and dropped by her office, she was wearing it!

The stuff that gets remembered, the thing that makes another person feel special, the gesture that makes life more fun—do more of that.

RULE #36: SEND A THANK-YOU EMAIL EVERY DAY

It's no secret that gratitude has a funny way of making life better. Expressing gratitude helps increase our resilience, strengthens our relationships and reduces stress and depression. It is truly impossible to be stressed and grateful all at once—try it!

One of my all-time favorite rules I've been living by for a long time now is to send an email of gratitude every single day. They're mostly only one or two sentences, but this habit makes me feel amazing and always helps lift my mood. It's also so fun to think of new people to send them to each day.

When I was first trying to make this a part of my daily routine, I popped a new appointment in my calendar (just for five minutes) every morning for three weeks. After that time, sending out a thank-you email became second nature to me, and it's something I do every single morning now when I first boot up my computer.

RULE #37: KNOW WHEN TO ASK FOR FAVORS

Life is an echo. What you send out, comes back.
What you sow, you reap. What you give, you get.
What you see in others, exists in you.

Zig Ziglar

When the pandemic hit, and our business got turned upside down, I had to call in lots of favors from people to help out. These had been relationships I'd been investing in for years, so every single person I asked for help was happy to jump in. I called in favors from speakers who we'd worked alongside to headline at our (now-digital) events. I called in favors from our people to take on work that wasn't part of their job descriptions, and I called in favors from friends and our members to support us in new ways. I'd been there for people over the years, and now they were happy to help in return.

When it comes to building relationships, we have to be really patient. And we've got to put in the hard yards. We've got to give, and give without the expectation that we're going to get anything back.

Have you ever noticed how it's inevitable to feel compelled to do something for someone who's done something for you, even if they haven't asked you to? This is called the Law of

Reciprocity, which simply means that when someone gives you something, you feel obligated to return the favor ("you scratch my back and I'll scratch yours"). The funny thing about this concept is that you often find yourself paying back their original favor at a much more generous level, even though no one asked you to.

Good networkers know this to be true, which is why they invest in their relationships all the time, even when there's no real pressing need. Life's easier when people are referring business to you and you're not the only one seeking it out.

I've found that the people who give without expectation are the ones who ultimately get ahead. We're in partnership with a company to co-produce our leadership programs. I've been so impressed with how gently yet skillfully they've been able to influence us and build a relationship with me and the stakeholders in our business. I didn't know them at all because my team had initiated the partnership, and my first contact was when they left a small gift and thoughtful handwritten card in my room at our annual conference. Since then, there have been multiple interactions and touch points with them—they're the first people to support us by booking into our events, and they always take a moment to say hi but not commandeer all my time, and they're just altogether supportive and lovely humans to deal with.

Contrast this with a company that recently sent some of their products to me (without asking) and then got very upset and irate when I wasn't comfortable posting about them on social media.

I can't stress strongly enough how important it is to have built your networks before you need to ask for favors. It'll make it that much easier for people to say yes when you've already done the work and built trust and credibility. We need to get into the habit of thinking about our networks just as we think about our bank accounts—we need to be constantly making deposits in other people's accounts, so that when the time comes for us to ask for some cash out (metaphorically speaking), they'll be more likely to hand over the check.

This is not being mercenary or selfish—it's just how life works. If you're a person who's generous and thinks of others and has put in the yards to build a relationship, then you're more likely to be given a yes when you next ask for a favor. The right mindset is needed here, though: you must give selflessly and without expectation for this banking relationship to work.

RULE #38: CHANGE THE QUESTION

I once had an assistant who made my life easier every day by changing the question. Instead of asking, "What do you want for lunch?" (which I never had an answer for) she'd ask, "Would you like a chicken sandwich, sushi, or a salad from Sweetgreen?"

You can do the same when scheduling a meeting. Instead of asking, "When suits you to meet up?" try this: "What works better for you? Mondays or Tuesdays?"

You get the idea. Humans are faced with a stupid amount of decisions each day, so change the question to make life easier for everyone.

RULE #39: BE NICE, OUT OF THE BLUE

This message recently hit my inbox from a past employee, Alana:

> Hey Em, I just wanted to say thank you for everything you have taught me in the past. One thing that has stuck with me for life is when you used to say, "you're never too senior to pick up a broom."
>
> I will carry that motto with me for my whole career. I value the impact you had on my early career life and I appreciate you.

How delighted do you think that made me feel?

Could you do the same for someone today? Who could you give a little bit of love/appreciation/gratitude to, completely out of the blue?

RULE #40: BE INTENTIONAL AND CONSISTENT WITH YOUR NETWORKING

We've all heard of six degrees of separation, which is the idea that any person on the planet can be connected to any other person on the planet through a chain of acquaintances that has no more than five links. Facebook upped the ante in 2015, reducing the number down from six and claiming that its users in the United States are now connected by an average of 3.46 people.

Given that now we can reach practically anyone we'd like through such a small number of contacts, why do so few people use this knowledge to really advance their careers and businesses? What do super-networkers know that we don't, and how can we learn to access this intelligence more?

The biggest difference I see between people who get a lot from their networks and those who don't is that the successful relationship-builders are those who are intentional with their networking. They work at it and they think about it all the time.

Yet while some people might be intentional, it doesn't necessarily make them effective. It might be worth thinking about those coffee meetings you invest in. Do they just lead to friendships and loose business connections, or are the people you're investing time in truly able to make an impact for you? A big factor in effective networking is that it's not about the quantity of your connections, it's the quality of those connections. I've never understood it when people brag about having 5,000 Facebook friends—I mean, who really cares?

To improve our networking, we have to be more strategic than collecting 5,000 Facebook buddies. An exercise that I've found really helpful is to spend a moment creating a list of your ten most powerful contacts. These people don't need to be well-known or powerful to anyone apart from you, but they're the people who come to mind when you think of power. They make stuff happen. They're well-connected themselves. You can rely on them, and they've proven their worth to you (in terms of opening doors or perhaps just being there to support you) time and time again.

One powerbroker for me is a gorgeous woman and Business Chicks member named Angela. Ange works in a senior executive role in a big business, and for the best part of the past decade, we've scratched each other's backs. If I need a corporate sponsor for an event, I'm comfortable asking Ange for the support. If it's a fit for her business and their current activities, she'll always support me. If I need some support with her buying a table or two at an event, she'll always try to make that happen too. In return, I've connected her with people she's needed to know, and I've gone into her business to give talks from time to time. It's wonderful having people like this in your corner, and I'm honored to also be in hers. I'd do anything for Ange.

Once you've identified your powerbrokers, get into the habit of picking one of them each week (on rotation) and doing something, anything, for them. Be sure to set this up in your calendar as a weekly task so you can ensure it gets done. This discipline is a beautiful way to work your network and stay in touch with people.

Another great way to keep in touch with the people who matter to you is just to drop them a short email from time to time. I do this regularly with our members. I'm never after anything from them, but a random, unexpected note to say, "I'm thinking of you" can go a long way toward making others feel great and building upon a relationship.

Remember also that sometimes the powerbroker isn't who you think it is. I'll give you an example. A lot of people think that I'm the powerbroker in a certain situation and that I can play a huge part in connecting them with our high-profile speakers, let's say. In lots and lots of cases I am, but for many more, it's actually one of my team members who has closer relationships with these people than I do. They're the ones dealing with them day in, day out, not me, so coming to me looking for an introduction can often be futile. Also, in a similar vein, the powerbroker can often be the high-profile person's business manager or assistant or even hair and make-up artist, as they're up in their face (literally!) all the time and know them really well. It's often not the talent themselves. Funny, huh?

My gorgeous mom makes an effort to come to our events in her hometown whenever she can. She's been attending our events for the past fifteen years and loves them. It's not always fun and glamorous for her, as they can be long days and I'm not around to entertain her (because I'm working!), but she always finds ways to entertain herself. Last year at one of our big summits, while I was busy meeting people and talking with members, she sat down in the foyer and got out her knitting. Cute. Mom has knitted squares for a charity in Africa for years—these squares get stitched together to make blankets for women and kids, and she's committed to knitting as many of these as she can whenever she gets a spare minute.

Now, most people might overlook a 65-year-old woman sitting there knitting quietly at a fast-paced, high-powered business event. You might think "she's not in my target demographic of businesswomen I need to meet" and walk right on by, wondering what she's even doing there. Last year, one of our members, Kim (who I'd never met), took the time to sit with my mom and have a chat with her for a good twenty minutes. She didn't know who my mom was, and Mom didn't tell her. Afterward, Mom raved about how kind Kim had been and told me all about Kim's incredible job at a gas company and how well she looked after her team and so on and so on. The next day I looked Kim up in our member database to thank her, and we've been in touch ever since. I'd do anything for Kim, given the kindness she showed my mother. At our events, most people think I'm the powerbroker, but I'm always pulled in different directions on those days and can't give the twenty minutes my mom did. I'm always going to take my mom's character judgment as gospel, and on this day she definitely played the powerbroker role.

RULE #41: SEEK OPPORTUNITY FOR OTHERS

I do believe that luck exists, but people choosing to share, support, connect, promote and raise others is how most things are actually accomplished.

Unknown

There's such magic to be found in championing others. In taking a stand for their greatness and intentionally looking for ways you can support them. I know I personally get such a kick from the times when I'm able to give someone else a leg up, and the more I do this, the more joy I get from it.

There was one time I wasn't available for a spot on a television show, so I thought long and hard about who I could recommend to the producers to replace me. I knew the opportunity could be game-changing for one of our members, so I referred finance expert Melissa Browne to them, and she went on to ace that appearance and become a regular commentator for the network too. During the pandemic I personally reached out to over fifteen of our members and subsequently helped them access a $10,000 government grant so they could stay in business. When my friend was raising money for her new company, I connected her with seven reasonably high-profile investors—one of whom went on to invest a sizable amount into her new business.

I've been on the receiving end of such kindness, too. I'll forever be grateful to my friend, author Sarah Wilson, who introduced me to her literary agent, whom I'm now lucky to call my agent too. And my dear bestie Narelle was the president of the Entrepreneurs Organisation and championed me to take over her role when her term was done, even though I was only twenty-four at the time.

It costs nothing to adopt this mindset and always be on the lookout for ways you can play a part, big or small, in another person's success.

RULE #42: DON'T DECIDE FOR ME

Often we let our biases stand in the way of what we feel another person is capable of doing. I've had this happen to me too many times to mention (and I'd hazard a guess that this more often than not happens to mothers over any other group of people). Someone will say to me, "We were thinking of you for this opportunity, but we know you have six kids, so we thought you might not want to travel for it." It also happened in our company a little while ago, with one of our team members deciding for a new employee that they wouldn't be up for a specific challenge because they were new to the business. I said to that person, "Don't take away the opportunity and decide for her! Give it to her and let her decide if she's up for it." Another friend of mine told me that, in her past workplace, her colleagues would often decide for her, "Oh, Emily is way too shy for that," but there were some instances where she would have jumped at the chance to try something.

Creating opportunities for others is great, particularly when you let them decide if they're up for it themselves.

RULE #43: SAY YES TO HELP!

A lot of us (me included) have been conditioned to give off we've-got-this vibes to everyone we know. I've always thought it's my job to help others and not to accept too much help in return. "Here to serve, here to serve" is my catchcry, and it's worked a charm in influencing others and building a really strong network of amazing people around me. The problem—which my younger self took a while to learn—is this: people want to help. People want to help, and when you deny them that opportunity, you've lost a chance to deepen your connection with them. It's also possible to be highly capable *and* to accept help, at the same time.

One of the best parts of living in America is that I usually have a ton of international visitors passing through (you know, when we're all allowed to travel, at least). These visitors often want to come and bask in the Isaacs family chaos for a few hours (why they'd ever want to do this is shocking to me, but still it happens a lot). Often our guests will ask if they can bring anything. My response used to be "No, we're totally fine, thanks anyway!" but I caught myself in the martyrdom cycle and started experimenting with a different answer. "Ooh yes, please!" I'll say now. "Bring some salted caramel Tim Tams, and I'll love you forever!"

These days, whenever our guests arrive with their goodies, we have a laugh together, and it creates a shared experience for us all to remember. When I used to say no, I denied them that chance to be generous, and I denied the opportunity for us to connect over a lovely gesture.

Same goes in your office or work environment. If someone offers up an "I'm going to Starbucks—you want one?," don't be a martyr if you really do want one! Be someone who creates positive energy and says, "Oh my goodness, yes! Thank you! I owe you one!"

When you say yes to accepting help, you say yes to making others feel great, too, and that's a beautiful way to make life that little bit more expansive.

write.

*I think writing well takes a little bit of talent
and a lot of hard work.*

Kristan Higgins

When I was a sophomore in high school, we had to get some work experience under our belt. Back then I had aspirations to work in the human resources department of a large corporation, so my dad sat down with me and helped me write application letters to a number of companies. I vividly remember him encouraging me to make my letter a little personal—to try to convey who I really was and have me stand out a little more than the next person who was also sending in their application.

As well as listing the leadership stuff I did at school and the casual job I held at the local restaurant, I remember coloring my application with phrases like "so this keeps me off the streets" and talking about my siblings fondly but also admitting "Of course they drive me up the wall at times." I guess my dad was trying to make me sound relatable and memorable.

It did feel a little goofy to me at the time, but it worked. I scored work experience at a pharmaceutical company and felt very special wearing my mom's jacket with shoulder pads and some black kitten heels into a fancy big office each day.

This experience taught me that revealing a little personality to try to get the attention of others can really get you places. When you pack your writing with the right amount of emotive language and understand your audience and their needs, you'll get your way more often than not.

If I had to rank career competencies in order of most important, I'd say influencing through writing would be way up there. It's a skill I've tried to learn as much as I can since my dad inspired me all those years ago—I went to courses on feature writing, courses on how to write blog posts, and other business communication writing workshops too. I had a writing mentor for a while as well. She was brutal and to-the-point with her feedback. I loved that. "No ego here—just help me get better, please," is what I'd say to her over and over again.

Obviously, most of our writing is done over email these days, so let's start there. To make your emails sing, no matter if they're small requests or large ones, keep these golden rules in mind, and you'll be well on your way to influencing effectively.

RULE #44: WHEN YOU PUNCH OUT YOUR EMAILS, DON'T FORGET YOUR PERSONALITY

I've got a friend everybody falls in love with. She's magnetic, funny, gregarious and always the life of the party. And yet when she emails, she's all formal and proper, and I'm always left thinking, "Why is she doing this? Where'd she go?" It's so weird that we think we have to turn into someone we're not and suddenly become altogether "professional" and a complete departure from who we really are.

Similarly, I once had a member on my team who insisted on being rigid and formal in all her emails. Every time an email came in from her, it was like we didn't know each other, and our relationship went back to square one each time. She'd start each message with "Dear Emma" or "Good morning, Emma" and sign them off with "Best wishes." Killed me. I only get called Emma when I'm in trouble or by people who don't know me; if my team feel as if they know me and have to be super formal, then we have a problem. I also saw it as a huge waste of time—if you write "Best wishes" as your sign-off in every email, then you're spending far too much time on emails. Being overly formal and proper actually alienates your audience and distances them from you, when the whole idea of communicating (in any form) is to bring people closer to you and your ideas.

I suffered this for a little while before addressing it with her, writing a quick email:

> Hey F!
>
> Two quick things . . .
>
> 1) Please call me Em. I don't know one team member in the history of Business Chicks who's called me anything different, and also, Emma is what I get called only when I'm in trouble ;-) (Am I in trouble???)
>
> 2) Please can you not write "Best wishes" as your email sign-off when you're emailing fellow team members? It's so formal and makes me think we've never met!!!!
>
> Thanks,
>
> Em

Immediately after that email was sent, F's writing started to improve. She explained to me that because I was the boss, she'd always thought she had to be more "professional" with me. I helped her see that there's always a way to remain professional and be respectful, but also write in a way that draws people in, not pushes them away.

Same thing goes for when you have to give a speech or get up in a meeting—be yourself! So many people forget to take themselves up onto that stage, thinking they have to be different or act in a certain way. Unless you're serving in a diplomatic role and meeting the Queen or the Prime Minister, people will be confused if you turn into someone completely different—and they'll see right through that lack of authenticity.

RULE #45: DON'T GIVE THE OTHER PERSON YOUR PROBLEMS

It's never appropriate to adopt a "woe is me" tone in your emails when you need someone to help you. Here's one as an example: "I've struggled for ages to make this dream a reality and have only just started paying myself a small salary, which is why I now need financial sponsorship." Instead, be positive and inspire others to see your vision, rather than complain about how hard it's been for you.

Perhaps a better way to attack this pitch might be: "I've been hustling hard these past few years and have built a little something I think you're going to love. It's going to take you and your smarts to take it to the next level, and I'd love to discuss working together to make that happen."

See how it's a little more uplifting and inspiring and might get your reader to sit up and want to know more? Being positive and not passing on your problems to others will always give you a head start in any pitch, request for help or offer to partner up . . . which brings me to my next tip.

RULE #46: WIIFM?

A common mistake made in emails is not thinking enough about the recipient. Most people are so focused on their problem or the ask that they fail to anticipate how the request might land with the person on the receiving end.

When trying to influence someone or convince them to do something for you, you need to commit this acronym to memory: WIIFM? It stands for "What's in it for me?" Whether you like it or not, people are waiting to get to the part where you explain what's in it for them. How will things be different for them if they say yes to this? How will it enhance their life? What problems will it solve for them? In other words, they're subconsciously asking, "what's in it for me, what's in it for me, what's in it for me?"

Take this one, for example.

A friend of mine, Kate, recently reached out to me. She said, "Hey, I have an ex-colleague who wants me to introduce you both. He runs trips overseas, and I think he wants to do this with Business Chicks now. You cool if I connect you?"

I responded with: "For sure, go for it. Not sure it's for us, but happy to chat with him all the same."

So Kate emails the guy, let's call him Josh: "Here's Emma, and I'll leave the two of you to it." Then Josh writes this:

> Hi Emma,
>
> When's a good time for you to chat, and what number can I get you on? Or perhaps we can do a Google Hangout when I'm back in the office April 15?
>
> Warm regards,
>
> Josh

Whoa, Josh! Cool your jets! I'm nowhere near ready to speak with you yet! Who even are you? What do you want? Why would I give you my number when I don't know you from a bar of soap?

I write back with this:

> Hi Josh,
>
> We might be jumping the gun a little! Maybe you can first give me an idea of what you're thinking? Kate mentioned you might want to partner up in some way? Just to let you know, we already have a bunch of experiences on the go (Leadership Programs in Africa, a

conference on Necker Island, Knowledge + Study Tours in New York and Los Angeles, etc.), so I'm not sure there's an appetite from our side and don't want to waste your time.

Love to hear more before we speak (I'm on deadline for a number of projects right now, meaning it'll be tricky to carve out time for a call), and in any case, I'm probably not your best bet from the business, but let's explore all the same!

Warmest,

Emma

So, let's deconstruct this. Where did Josh go wrong in his approach? First, he assumed that I was interested and would want to make time for a call (when really, I had no available information about his pitch, and also, I'm an absolute time ninja, so I don't just go jumping on calls with random strangers). Second, he gave me zero context, so I was shooting blind with what he wanted to discuss (thank goodness for Kate, who at least gave me a small inkling before she made the connection).

Josh's response could have been something like this:

Hey Emma!

Great to e-meet you. Any friend of Kate's is a friend of mine!

I know we haven't met, but I've admired your work from afar and really feel there's a synergy in our businesses and values. I think what you've created with Business Chicks is magic, and I believe I can play a small part in helping you make it even better.

Our expertise is in curating travel adventures that combine networking with social impact. The best part of our work is seeing what happens for participants when they experience one of our trips. I can only imagine that one of your business challenges (as it is with many of the other amazing membership organizations we're lucky enough to work with) is how to continuously engage your members, and over the past fifteen years, we've mastered the art of this.

I can see you're in partnership with other brands to execute similar experiences, but really believe we can provide something completely unique, new and fresh for you. And we can do it in a way that won't take up any of your or your team's time. Would you be open to a super sharp fifteen-minute introductory call (or even a quick proposal of sorts) as to how we might work together?

Thanks so much, Emma—really excited to explore this with you!

Best wishes,

Josh

So what do you think? It's much warmer, it's non-intrusive, it doesn't make assumptions that I'm ready to talk, and overall, it shows Josh has put more care into his response. His original real email left me thinking he was just trying to sell me something, but this example would have made me feel that he took the time to really lay out a case for why I might want to have a conversation with him. The improved email includes a few tricks that would bring me a little closer to him and his pitch: he uses flattery without sounding too sucky, he sounds like he's done his research, he refers to my possible business challenges without overdoing it, and overall he just makes it more about us than him.

Had he come forward with that sort of approach, as opposed to being brash and assumptive, I would have been more inclined to take him up on his offer of a call or at least connect him with the right person in the business to take the call.

On a more day-to-day basis, you can use the same thinking when dealing with teammates, suppliers or anyone else you need to deal with. Make it clear that there's a reason you're reaching out. Make it clear that you possibly have a solution that will solve something for them. And keep the focus on them and their needs—not you and yours.

RULE #47: DEAL WITH POTENTIAL OBJECTIONS

When you're writing to influence others, always be thinking about what your audience might be subliminally objecting to while reading your pitch.

In the example email from Josh, he does a great job of dealing with a lot of possible objections . . .

Possible objection I don't want to do this because my team is already stretched with their workload.
Response "And we can do it in a way that won't take up any of your or your team's time."

Possible objection We're already doing this type of thing.
Response "I can see you're in partnership with other brands to execute similar experiences, but really believe that we can provide something completely unique, new and fresh for you."

Possible objection I don't have time for this.
Response "Would you be open to a super sharp fifteen-minute introductory call (or even a quick proposal of sorts) as to how we might work together?"

You always want to put yourself in the shoes of your recipient, rather than just see life from your own perspective.

RULE #48: BE PATIENT

Sending an email might be the most important task on your list, but reading it probably won't be top priority for the person you're reaching out to. Don't send it marked as high importance, and don't call to see if they received your email. It's appropriate to follow up, say, a week later if they haven't responded, but give people the time they need to reply.

If it's been a week or two since your approach, it might be okay to forward the message again with "Hi Claire, appreciating how busy your schedule is, I just wanted to pop this to the top of your inbox. Really hope to hear from you when you get the chance!" I'm actually grateful when people do this to me, because often the only reason I haven't responded is that time has simply slipped away, and before I know it, that email is buried under fifty others.

RULE #49: GRAMMAR MATTERS. SPELLING DOES TOO.

This rule seems so basic, yet it's regularly broken. Spend time working out your "yours" from your "you'res" and your "theirs" from your "they'res." If this is an area you struggle with, then make sure you've got a software program like Grammarly helping you through.

I don't know about you, but if an email hits my inbox with a "Hi Emma, hope your well," I'm pretty much immediately switched off and can't get past that first sentence. Anyone else with me here?

RULE #50: LEAVE NO ROOM FOR CONFUSION

When you're pitching something, no matter whether it's by email or via a more creative offline method, the person should in no way be left wondering what you're asking for. Your pitch should be clear and concise and to the point. Your end goal is not to impress others with your writing skills, but rather to influence them effectively to get the outcome you want.

Just before I wrote my first book, I received this email:

Dear Emma

I'm xxx, a Director at xxx, one of the country's largest independent book publishers. I'd love to talk to you about the idea of publishing a book.

I firmly believe there is a large audience who would love to read your story and your thoughts on life, business and beyond.

If this idea is of interest and you'd like to explore it a little more, perhaps you could call or email me. My cell is xxx.

I hope to hear from you soon,

Best wishes, xxx

It's brilliant because it leaves precious little to the imagination. I know what she's asking for, she hasn't wasted my time, she's been kind and genuine (and used a bit of flattery—remember that tactic never goes astray), and most importantly, she's been straight to the point and hasn't wasted my time.

RULE #51: EFFECTIVE EMAILS NEED TO BE PERSONALIZED

It might not surprise you to learn that I'm not a fan of blanket pitch emails—sure, you can take a chunk of copy from a template and reuse it, but make sure your messages are addressed personally and have some personal banter in there at the start to show that you care and have thought the pitch through. How many emails do you read that start with "Hi there" or "Hello" and nothing else? It's an almost-instant way to know that either someone hasn't taken the time to research who they're pitching to, or it's an automated approach.

You'll have a lot more success if you can tailor your pitches individually and take the time to research who the decision maker might be. You can call and ask a company this, or you can go to their website, or do a quick LinkedIn search. If you can't find the right contact, at least start your message with "I understand you're most likely not the right person for this, so I'd love to ask for your help in getting it into the hands of the right team member who handles this stuff." This shows a level of respect and thoughtfulness.

And never, ever send your pitch to four different people in the same business, hoping one sticks. What'll happen is that all of those four people will think that someone else will respond to your email, and then invariably no one does. Besides, it's just lazy and impolite to do this—and the team members will likely talk and see through your tactics too.

RULE #52: A RELATIONSHIP DOESN'T END BECAUSE SOMEONE SAID NO

Remember that lovely, to-the-point email I received from that prospective publisher for my first book? Ultimately, we decided not to go with her, but that wasn't the end of it. We've since gone on to refer her multiple clients who are more suited to her publishing house than the one we're contracted to, and she's become a loyal Business Chicks member too. We often go to her for advice, and she does the same with us. Her succinct, well-considered initial approach was the start of a working friendship we're happy to have.

And what if someone says no to you? For most of us, rejection is a real confidence-crusher, but you can also use it as fuel to make your next move.

Jamie Kern Lima is the founder of IT Cosmetics, the largest luxury make-up brand in the US. I love hearing about Jamie's rejection stories because of the sheer volume of times she was turned down by a retailer or an investor or even a family member who thought her idea was too wild. Hers is a classic "overcoming-all-odds" story, and instead of closing the book on those relationships when someone said no, she would instead keep trying in her own sneaky ways. "I would literally follow up with an email thanking them and saying, I can't wait for the day that we're in your stores." She would also reach out every time IT launched a new product or garnered some media, sending a note about that too. Over time, she started to receive more yeses, and it was that persistence that eventually paid off in a big way—a few years ago, Jamie sold her business to L'Oreal for $1.2 billion.

lead.

The old way of hustling saw people as expendable and easily replaceable. They were there to do a job, and they should stay in that system and be grateful for their employment. The only bit of this that I agree with is the gratitude part. We should all be very grateful for our work, for a job, for a career—that will never change—but the new hustle puts people first and has them sitting at the top of any decision that gets made.

I've seen firsthand what happens when you try to honor your people and see them as your greatest asset. When you continually think about how they're doing, if they're enjoying themselves, if your culture could be better in any way. It's so important to keep these ideas at the forefront of your mind so you keep improving every day.

The way to keep improving each day is to work on your leadership skills—to work out how you can inspire others and keep your people focused and happy. Because leadership is so important to us at Business Chicks, we made sure "Above all, inspire" made our list of core values. So let's start there . . .

RULE #53: ABOVE ALL, INSPIRE

Management is about persuading people to do things
they do not want to do, while leadership is about inspir-
ing people to do things they never thought they could.

Steve Jobs

Leaders, listen up. Your number one job is to help your people enjoy the time they spend at work. That's it. If I had to pick one reason why you're in that seat, that'd be the one I'd choose. You might think your number one job is to get through your workload and your meetings and your projects and get a gold star at the end of the day, but it's not. A leader's role first and foremost is to serve their people and help them be successful and happy at work.

So how do we do this? To start with, you make yourself fun and enjoyable to be around. You make yourself as predictable as possible—and by predictable, I don't mean boring. You should be anything but boring. Your aim is to be an inspiring human! Being inspiring doesn't mean being charismatic and upbeat every minute of the day, but it means your people should know what they're going to get with you. The worst leaders, in my opinion, are those with whom you have to pick your moments. Are they in a good mood? Okay, cool, now's a good time—or, uh-oh, looks like they're in a state. Can't approach them now.

Think for a moment about the productivity we lose trying to predict a leader's mood like this. The time we spend walking on eggshells and maneuvering around people who we should be able to approach directly, whenever we need. It's debilitating for a business and for the people inside of it.

A truly inspirational leader does a few things really well. First, they know that enthusiasm is one of the greatest gifts you can give the world. They answer the phone with a smile, genuinely happy to hear from the caller. They hug or shake hands with gusto. They laugh unabashedly at the joke and at themselves too. They stride into a room or a meeting looking like there's no place they'd rather be. They attack every task with delight, confident they're going to win at it, or at least learn something if they fail. Inspirational leaders set the tone and the mood and, in doing so, set an example for everyone else to follow.

Inspirational leaders are radical optimists. They see the positive part of every situation and the best in every person. They believe in a better future, a better world, a better experience for us all. They radiate possibility and urge us to find a better way. They encourage us to think a little differently until magic emerges.

Inspirational leaders make the unpopular and tough decisions so their vision can be realized and are unapologetic about knowing what they need and want.

Inspirational leaders don't micro-manage. They don't nitpick. They don't talk behind people's backs. They speak with intent, choosing their words carefully, knowing how powerful language can be.

Inspirational leaders make you feel as though you hung the moon—if you find one to work alongside, you should stick around until the stars are lined up too.

RULE #54: TURN ON THE CHARISMA

If one of the main factors of amazing leadership is being inspiring, then it'd make a lot of sense for us to pay attention to how we become more inspirational. I've always found that the most inspiring people I know have worked out how to dial up one trait in particular: charisma.

You can sense a charismatic person from the moment they enter a room. The energy automatically lifts. They cause us to stop whatever it is we're doing and give our full attention. In a split second, they have us turning our heads as if their presence just signaled something special is about to happen. The charms of a charismatic person are intoxicating, and it's unlikely you'll be able to look away as they draw you into their world and make you forget (momentarily) about anything else.

When we worked with actress and entrepreneur Kate Hudson, she invited me and my CEO, Olivia, out to dinner to get to know one another. Kate had just arrived in Australia from the US the day before, so she was jetlagged and (unbeknown to all of us at the time) also in the first trimester of her pregnancy. Unless she's immune to those early hormones (which is unlikely . . . I'm yet to meet a newly pregnant woman who doesn't want to spend the majority of her time lying horizontal at any opportunity), she must have been completely exhausted. Anyone of less substance might have canceled the dinner, but not Kate.

Liv and I were the first to arrive at the restaurant that night. We ordered a drink and stood chatting, waiting for the rest of the group to arrive. We settled in and became so ensconced in conversation that we were caught a little unawares by Kate when she walked in. Well, she didn't really walk in, she floated in. And as she floated in, time stopped. I've relived that moment a few times over now, studying what happened and what made Kate so charismatic. Above anything else, I'd say it was her ability to be completely present with us all. Before she looked around the room and took it all in, she took us in. She walked straight up to Liv and me, introducing herself warmly and not breaking eye contact for a second. There was not one ounce of either arrogance or uneasiness—it felt as if she was grateful to be there and grateful to be spending time with us.

Over dinner, Kate held center court, telling elaborate stories and making us all laugh. She didn't put on airs, and she was as comfortable teasing herself as she was with teasing others. She asked lots of questions and remained interested in our answers.

The night flew by, and when she left, we all looked at each other as if to say, "What just happened here?"

A few years ago, I met Olivia Fox Cabane, who's an expert in charisma. She wrote the book *The Charisma Myth* and teaches the subject at Stanford and Berkeley's Business School too.

Olivia believes that while not all of us are born with the charisma of Kate Hudson, we can certainly learn the skill.

The first way to become more charismatic is through our presence. Presence is all about being in the moment, just as Kate was with us. Olivia says that if you find your attention slipping while speaking to someone, refocus by centering yourself. It's important you master the skill of being present, as you'll make everyone else more comfortable around you and make them feel as though they matter.

Olivia says that power is the second way we can get more charisma. In this context, power is achieved by taking away self-doubt and assuring yourself that you belong and that you've earned your place in that room. Have you ever been at a conference or a networking event and met someone who sort of looks like they're a little scared to be there, almost hiding behind someone else so you don't notice them? This is the opposite of exhibiting power. Power is all about being confident and owning your successes and not letting your self-limiting beliefs get in the way. Powerful people make us feel at ease, and they encourage us to act more confidently too.

If you can nail power and presence, you'll be well on your way, but here are six other tips to make like Ms. Hudson and level up your charisma.

Walk in like you own the room Shoulders back, head up and a big smile on your dial is how you should enter every room. Don't confuse this approach with arrogance, though. I'm not saying you need a swagger here, I'm talking about a genuine happiness to be in whichever room it is that you're walking into. Don't shrink yourself, don't make yourself smaller, don't apologize for walking into that room, don't cover yourself up by folding your arms or holding your handbag across your body—walk into that room with open body language, a strong posture and a good dose of confidence (even if you're making it up a little).

Ask lots of questions Charismatic people ask lots of questions in order to get the other person talking. Asking questions demonstrates that you're interested and that you care, and it means you can learn something about them too. The fastest way we can build our charisma is to get the other person talking, as, let's face it, most people love to talk—especially if it's about themselves!

Deeply listen Like, *really* listen. So many of us are having conversations where we're not really in them. You'll build your charisma when you can show people that you're intently listening to whatever it is that they're sharing with you. Forget about planning what you want to say next, and truly focus in on what they are saying. When you're actively listening like this, you need to avoid interrupting at all costs; summarize and repeat back what you have heard, and observe body language to give you an extra level of understanding. Active listening is a helpful skill for all of us to develop. It helps you truly understand what people are saying in conversations and meetings (not just what you want to hear or think you hear). Come to think of it, it's a pretty darn useful skill for our personal relationships too . . .

Nonverbal listening While you're deeply listening (and not talking!), give nonverbal cues: nod your head, frown, smile, look surprised or amused or horrified or however the situation calls for you to react . . . Patti Wood, a body language expert, says that in a face-to-face interaction with just one person you can exchange up to 10,000 nonverbal cues in less than one minute. "You cannot consciously control all that communication, so it can be much more telling than the few words you could exchange in the same amount of time," Patti says. Nonverbal listening includes your body language, so stay open, uncross your arms and lightly touch the person, but only if you feel it's absolutely appropriate and welcome—if not, don't attempt this at all. Sometimes though, where appropriate, a soft touch on the arm or a high five is a great way to build rapport and lift your charisma.

Never give advice Want to know the fastest way to drop your charisma quotient? Tell people what to do. Charismatic people know that advice-giving is mostly futile and really only ever makes the person dishing it out feel better about themselves. Most people are venting just to be heard, not to ask what you think they should do. Unless they specifically ask you for advice, don't offer it up.

Pay attention to your voice Ever noticed how a yawn creeps in or you find yourself drifting off, wondering what's for dinner, when you have to listen to someone with a monotone voice? Do your best to get some expression in your voice when you speak, and pay attention to the volume you're speaking at too. Try to intonate a little as well: that is, speak louder when required and softer when appropriate. And never mumble.

One great piece of advice I heard somewhere is to smile when you answer the phone. The whole tone of the human voice changes when you are smiling. It is totally noticeable (even though subconsciously, most likely) to the caller, and it sets the tone for the rest of the conversation.

Bonus hot tip If I could ask you to please remove one phrase from your vocabulary and never, ever use it again, it'd be this: "You look tired." I mean, is there a more disconcerting and demoralizing thing to have someone tell you? If you look tired, chances are you feel exhausted and you're very much aware of how that's showing on your face. To have someone tell you is only going to make you feel worse, whereas the aim with any rapport/relationship-building is to leave the other person feeling better!

RULE #55: HAVE TOUGH CONVERSATIONS

I want you to think about your leadership in the same way I'm guessing you want your toilet paper to be: tough but soft.

A person who nails this kind of leadership is my friend Jane Wurwand. Jane founded the skincare brand Dermalogica, and she is one of my favorite humans ever. I admire her for several thousand reasons, and over the past few years as I've gotten to know her, she's become a role model and mentor to me. It'd be hard to find a leader I want to emulate more than Jane. She is someone whose leadership style leaves you with little question of where you stand and what she expects from you, and everywhere she turns, she seems to get the best from people.

One time, when Jane was the guest speaker at one of our events, someone asked her about her approach to firing people. Jane answered with one of the most profound yet practical answers I've heard, and it's one that's stayed with me since.

I think we'd all agree that laying someone off from their job is one of the toughest things a manager can be asked to do. Jane takes a more upbeat approach to the task, though, saying it need not be as distressing as it mostly is. Jane's approach always starts by inviting the person into her office and asking them four simple words: "Are you happy here?"

Jane says one of two things will happen from there. The first is that the person will answer that they're "very happy, and everything's fine." When this happens, Jane responds with something like, "Well, you don't seem happy, and I'm not really seeing it in your work or your attitude," and this then leads to a conversation about how to fix the issue. She'll tell that person they need to sit down with their manager and figure out what they need to focus on to get their work back on track in the next thirty or sixty days.

The second reaction Jane receives from employees is an admission that no, they're not happy. That person will often vent about why they're not happy (Jane always listens and provides that space for them to share openly), and then when they're done, Jane thanks them for their honesty and acknowledges that their unhappiness has been noticed within the business. And then, just like in the first scenario, she'll suggest working with their manager, but this time on how the company can help find them a job that makes them happy (but not in her business!).

It's a straightforward and fair approach that works for everyone, and again, leaves the person in no question of where they stand and what the path forward should be. Jane for president, seriously.

Another leader who subscribes to the tough but soft approach is Arianna Huffington. A core value for her Thrive Global company is "compassionate directness." Arianna says creating an environment that encourages continuous and honest feedback is essential for allowing a business and its people to grow.

"When a culture of compassionate directness is created, people respond. They want to be empowered to make their voices heard, and they want to be respected enough to get the honest feedback they need to realize their full potential," Arianna says.

The problem is that we're too squeamish with being given it straight. We spend far too much time skirting around the real issues and not wanting to hurt people's feelings. Giving permission for your people to be "compassionately direct" is, in my opinion, a really useful philosophy we could all learn a lot from. It'd save so much time and emotional angst if we could get to a point of honesty and directness, served up with a side order of compassion, of course.

Having tough conversations at work isn't always as easy as Jane and Arianna make it look. I admire any outlier who appreciates it's just part of the leader's job to start and handle difficult conversations.

Having a tough conversation requires two ingredients: confidence and bravery on the part of the person who instigates the chat, and an openness and willingness to accept feedback from the person on the receiving end. And the good news is that you can control at least one part of this equation. Avoiding the conversation is not helpful for anyone. So why do we find it so hard to have challenging conversations?

In our obsession to be liked, we fear any situation that may place us in danger of jeopardizing our likability. We believe that having a tough conversation diminishes the way we're perceived at work. We trade short-term uneasiness for long-term dysfunction, hoping the situation won't get any worse before we can find the guts to address what's really going on.

Some workplaces don't do anything to help the situation. Perhaps the culture of your organization leans toward passive-aggressiveness, and you just can't see the precedence of people leading confidently. We need our workplaces to encourage bravery in dealing with what needs to be said, without people fearing they'll be reprimanded or thought less of.

Healthy role modeling is what's required here, so think about who your Jane might be that can help you build more expertise, and then practice, practice, practice.

RULE #56: THE 8-MINUTE PERFORMANCE REVIEW

I think it's very important to have a feedback loop,
where you're constantly thinking about what you've done
and how you could be doing it better.

Elon Musk

Many managers struggle to give effective feedback. Mostly they do one of two things—they wait too long to give feedback, or they get so scared of giving negative feedback and hurting a team member's feelings that they don't give it at all.

I've never been a massive fan of the annual performance review process as it stands in most companies. In fact, a Gallup survey revealed that only 14 percent of employees say that their performance review actually inspired them to improve.

By my way of thinking, every single day should be a performance review of sorts between leaders and their teams. Team members should feel comfortable putting ideas forward and giving suggestions as to how the leader can improve, in the same way the leader should feel that their team members are open to receiving feedback. If feedback is saved up for one day a year, achievements and areas for improvement are things of the past, and it's mostly disheartening for team members to have them raised so long after the fact.

Last year, I gave a performance review to one of my closest team members and, well, it lasted eight minutes. This team member regularly tells me what I can do better (I try to be a receptive leader who listens, is amenable to coaching and wants to improve)—and I tell her when I'm not happy with something or can see a gap she can't see. On the day of the performance review, we went into a room and I said to her, "You know all I have to say because we've lived through it together and I tell you every day. I know your trigger points and I can see you're working on them, and I'm super pleased with how far you've come. You've applied yourself and you're moving forward and you are such an asset to us, and I'm grateful for that. I have no surprises I'm saving up here for you. Now, what would you like to say?" This team member had similar responses, and we were able to move on to the rewards and recognition part of the conversation (which, by the way, should also not be saved up for just one day of the year— you should be using every day as an opportunity to reward and recognize your people in whatever ways you can).

Our chat was productive and effective, and it took up only eight minutes of our day. I've never been a fan of filling up space just because it's available to us. I could have taken up a full hour doing that performance review just so we could have looked like we were "working," but "working" to me means being efficient, it means being radically honest, and it means not wasting time.

Feedback should never be saved up for the annual performance review. It should be an ongoing conversation, without surprise, between you and your people or you and your line manager as to how they can do better, and how they feel you can do better.

RULE #57: BE ONE STEP AHEAD

Want to know the secret to keeping good talent on your team? Be one step ahead always. Anticipate their needs. Look out for when they're showing signs of boredom or apathy and try to offer their next stretch project. If they're entering a new life phase (maybe becoming a parent, let's say), anticipate what they might be thinking and feeling and come up with solutions before they've even asked for them. If you get a hunch that they might be starting to look for a role elsewhere, send them a note saying how much they're valued, or offer a small pay incentive. Do whatever it takes, and always be one step ahead.

It pays to look ahead, too, no matter where you are in the organization. Is your boss thinking of moving on? Is there (another!) restructure in the cards? A change in direction that will affect your area? Might the company be in some financial trouble? Perhaps the Christmas presents were a little smaller than the year before? By keeping your finger on the pulse, you'll always be one step ahead.

RULE #58: LET THEM OFF

You've heard the saying "Get the right people on the bus," which was made famous by Jim Collins back in 2001 in his book *Good to Great*. Getting the right people on the bus means making sure you have awesome people riding along with you as you build your company into the force it can be. Metaphorically, these people need to be the right ones, and they need to be sitting in the right seats before the bus can begin its journey.

Sounds easy, but of course it's more difficult in practice. Hiring great talent takes time and effort, and it requires you to have an X factor that puts your brand ahead of your competition.

I've made so many mistakes in my business when it comes to people, and most of these mistakes come down to keeping the wrong people on the bus for far too long. I've wanted to do the "right thing" and be the "nice person" and keep my fingers and toes crossed that they improve or the situation would somehow work itself out. I've been around the block enough now to know that neither situation ever really eventuates. If you know someone isn't right, you need to ring that bell on the bus signaling for it to stop, and then you need to gently escort them off it.

When entrepreneur and author Marie Forleo spoke for Business Chicks, she said, "It's not always about who you hire. It's about who you fail to fire. Those people will ruin your business."

Amen, sister.

RULE #59: REMOVE THE PEAS

As a kid, I hated peas. I'd stash them in a glass of milk or down my socks when no one was looking. I'd put them on my sister's plate when Mom and Dad weren't watching and find them in my pockets days after, too. One time at school we had to give a speech and were allowed to choose any topic in the world. The other kids chose subjects like the Vietnam War and Newton's laws of motion. I chose to talk about how much I hated peas.

Stay with me here. There's a reason I'm talking about peas.

If you're a leader, your job is to remove the peas. It's to get rid of the friction or the pain points or the frustrations that your team members experience at work each day.

Does their equipment work well? Are they comfortable? Do the rules of the company make their life (at work) harder or easier? What can you do to support them? All of these questions are important ones for leaders to consider. If you can build a reputation for serving your people and trying to remove the roadblocks that make parts of their work frustrating, you'll be well on the way to gaining their trust and earning your credibility.

I was in my office recently and walked by the desk of one of the team members. This team member is responsible for doing tasks that take up a bit of space: receiving all the mail and packages that come in for the team each day, plus managing all the outgoing mail, too, and she always seems to be sorting receipts and paperwork as well. There were piles of stuff everywhere, and while it looked reasonably organized, you couldn't see the top of her desk under all those piles. If the lack of available space was giving me a small amount of anxiety from just walking past it, then I could imagine she might be finding this quite frustrating. I asked her, "Is this setup working for you?," and she said, "No! No matter how I try to organize myself, I never seem to have enough room." I went back to my computer, did a quick search online and ordered a small bookshelf that she could place beside her desk to organize all that paperwork. She was super grateful that I'd taken the time to find a solution and even asked her about it in the first place, saying, "I was just so in it that I couldn't see that I needed a little more space, and anyway didn't know that this was available to me, so thought I just had to suffer through with the one desk." If you're a leader, learn to tune in to what makes work frustrating for your people, and do what you can to remove those frustrations, no matter how big or small they are.

Don't think of yourself as a leader quite yet? Think again. Even if you don't have the leader title, you can still play a huge part in making work fun for you and your teammates. Instead of waiting for your manager to remove frustrations for you and your colleagues, also be on the lookout for problems you can solve for others. Get known as the positive, upbeat colleague who wants to help make work better for everyone, and you'll be well on your way to getting that title you deserve.

RULE #60: PROTECT THE MAVERICKS

BE TOO MUCH. And do not apologize for it.

Luvvie Ajayi Jones

I've always been drawn to mavericks. Mavericks think differently, act differently, and in most cases piss people off. They're the ones willing to speak their minds, offer up an unthought-of perspective and generally do lots of cutting: cutting the crap and cutting to the chase and in the process cutting some relationships too.

Mavericks are often misunderstood, and they can be hard work, but every extraordinary organization needs them. Without them, a company remains ordinary (just like vanilla ice cream) and won't ever be able to truly find a point of difference.

No one can argue that mavericks haven't changed the world. Dame Jane Goodall listened to not many people apart from herself, studying chimpanzees and creating a perhaps peerless conservation legacy in the process. Malala Yousafzai championed girls' education and wouldn't let the Taliban silence her. Greta Thunberg continues to insist world leaders listen to her demands for immediate climate change action. As for business mavericks, we wouldn't have our iPhones and our MacBooks without Steve Jobs, and our VPL (visible panty line) disappeared thanks to Spanx's Sara Blakely. The renewable energy space wouldn't be as exciting if Elon Musk hadn't done his thing with solar power and electric cars and space travel, and if you've ever flown Virgin, you owe that experience to perhaps the original maverick, Richard Branson.

One of my favorite mavericks is Luvvie Ajayi Jones. Luvvie calls herself a "fear-fighter" and wants us all to become one too. In her latest book, *Professional Troublemaker*, she writes, "When we talk about people being their full selves and how a lot of people are afraid of it, it's not that people don't want to show up as themselves. It's that they know that when they show up in their full splendor, they will be judged for it. Being ordinary and unremarkable is hardly a life goal, but we are often scared into being that way."

Mavericks are relentless in their pursuit of their goals. They take no prisoners. They don't let roadblocks stand in the way, simply side-stepping them and carrying on. They shun old ways of thinking and are always curious about how to do things better. They're ruthless at imagining new futures, being doggedly creative and taking the risks that others don't dare to.

Mavericks are misunderstood and often struggle in companies where the culture is "let's all be nice to each other and relate and always agree and never rock the boat." The problem with this type of culture is that we're so busy relating to one another and keeping the peace that we miss the opportunity for critical thinking and extraordinary ideas. Without a maverick to interrupt the pleasantness, companies can never exploit greatness.

If you're the maverick in your company, keep going. We need you and your tenacity. If you're not the maverick, please don't try to tame them or drive them out. Protect the maverick at all costs. Your company's life depends on it.

RULE #61: DO MORE DELEGATING

> *Deciding what not to do is as important*
> *as deciding what to do.*
>
> Jessica Jackley, co-founder of Kiva

If I turn the clock back twenty years, I remember a version of myself that hated delegating. It always felt like I'd failed if I had someone else do what I should have been able to do myself. Thank goodness I got over that way of thinking—now anyone who knows me well will tell you that I'm a total boss when it comes to delegating. This is mainly because I don't have the time to be in the detail like I used to, and I've also realized that most people can do so many things better than me anyway.

If you're a leader and not yet convinced that delegating is a key skill you need to focus on developing, let me try to win you over. By delegating effectively, you give your team more confidence, and you empower them to do their best. When you delegate well, you're showing others that they're important to you and that you believe in their abilities. Delegating tasks to your team also builds engagement, as you're showing trust and silently sending a message that says, "You've got this."

Here's how I went from "I've got to do it all myself" to becoming a delegating pro:

I got specific Ronald Reagan, former president of the United States, was known as being a master delegator. It's widely reported that to get what he needed done he simply had a knack for asking his people to handle it. A key to Reagan's skill was being specific with his requests, and this is something we should take on too. Instead of asking, "Will you send me that report?," you should be even more specific and leave no room for ambiguity, saying instead: "I need you to please email me the final sales numbers for Q1 by four today." If you can master being really specific and clear with your communication, you'll make it easier for yourself and easier for your people to meet you with what you need.

I learned to let go In my experience of watching people struggle to delegate well, I've seen it mostly comes down to one foundational problem: not being able to let go. People who struggle with delegation generally want to be in control, and as we all know, so much of our work and our lives is, at some level, uncontrollable. Giving up the need to control is a beautiful feeling and means we get to focus on other things and trust other people at the same time. I've really practiced letting go of situations and problems in my home, and that's been a great teacher in delegation: I can be sitting working and hear one of my kids fall over and let out that sort of cry that means they've hurt themselves. If it's at a time when I have someone else looking after them, I've trained myself not to jump up and run to them (unless the cry is one where I can just tell it's going to result in a hospital visit— then of course I'll go running). My point is that I've learned to let go and not be the linchpin in every situation at home and at work. Others can and should be trusted to do their jobs well.

I never set anyone up to fail It would be unfair to delegate a task to a person who's not up to it. That's just a waste of your time and theirs, and it's a sure-fire way to make someone feel inept. I've learned to delegate to people's strengths, and I've also learned that we shouldn't delegate to members on our teams just because they have the lightest workload or others are too busy. I've learned that your most effective people are those who seem to be able to take on as much as you're willing to trust them with (provided they're not completely overwhelmed, of course).

I use delegation as a training technique Delegating can make for a great opportunity to teach someone a new skill. You'd start the conversation with: "I really need you to take this on, as it's becoming too much for me and I know you'd be great at it. Can I show you how to get it done?" Too often leaders delegate without giving the proper training and instructions and then get frustrated if the task isn't up to their standards. When you invest the time in your people and show them the way, everyone wins: they get to learn a new skill, and it's one less thing on your to-do list as well.

I practiced over and over until it felt more comfy If you aren't at ease with delegating, practice starting with smaller tasks until you've built your confidence a little. Also start with the low-risk tasks that aren't business-critical so if it goes awry, you can step in and get things back on track.

RULE #62: BECOME AN APPRECIATION EXPERT

It's pretty simple: your workplace will become happier when people feel appreciated and valued.

I think I'm pretty good at this, but I've tripped up many times in the past, and I still stumble from time to time in doing my best to show my people I care. For example, I wanted to buy each member of my team a plant for their desk at home recently (I'm a crazy plant lady and get so much joy from my planties, so I thought they might too). I tracked down all their addresses and then started writing personalized messages, sending the plants out before I realized that the plant place didn't deliver to some of the areas where our team members lived. Oops. I messed up, but I'm human, and I had the best intentions. I felt bad about this, but also resolved to make it up to the people who missed out.

Plants aside, the thing is this: your people need appreciation from you. They need to know they matter, and it's your job to tell them that, over and over again. Where it gets tricky is that they need it in different ways.

When I was much younger, I enthusiastically read the book *The Five Love Languages* by Gary Chapman. Revolutionary! I'm sure you've read it or at least heard of it, but the basic premise of the book is that there are five love languages. Chapman says we all speak in a primary love language, and we have secondary ones too. The secret to a great relationship is to work out the love language of your partner and communicate in that language as much as you can.

Chapman later teamed up with Paul White to write *The Five Languages of Appreciation in the Workplace*, which I've found to be an extraordinary resource. I'll often refer back to it when I'm struggling with how best to motivate someone on my team.

The five languages of appreciation are the same as the love languages:

1. Words of affirmation
2. Quality time
3. Acts of service
4. Tangible gifts
5. Appropriate physical touch

My CEO, Olivia, won't mind me sharing this learning experience with you. Liv and I have worked together on and off since we were in our early twenties when she came into my first company (a recruitment agency) looking for a job to support herself through college. Recognizing her brilliance in about the first thirty seconds of our meeting, I snapped her up for my company instead of releasing her onto the temp market like she initially wanted.

Liv and I are often mistaken for sisters and always know what the other is thinking without either of us having to use words. She's a fierce leader, often wearing her heart on her sleeve, highly passionate (she's half Sicilian, after all), and she's also loyal to the core.

Given I know her so well, you'd think I'd have worked out by now how to tell her how much I appreciate all she does for me, our team and the company. And I really have tried over all these years. I'd tell her all the time how awesome she was, and I'd write to her all the time telling her what a great job she was doing. I always did my best to thank her when I noticed something she'd done well. I always felt like I was highly intentional with this gratitude—I put a lot of effort into it and really tried my best to thank her often, and I'd feel like crap and it would really bother me when I knew I hadn't shown my appreciation for a while.

Still, every now and then something would come up and she'd tell me she didn't feel appreciated. What? I just couldn't understand it. I could pull up ten emails from the past few weeks where I'd been highly demonstrative with saying how well she was doing and how much I appreciated it. In my mind, I'd remember the gifts I'd bought for her over the years or that voucher to her favorite store. I totally appreciated her!

For ages I thought the problem was with her, and once I said to her, "Liv, I actually can't tell you any more than I am about what a good job you're doing. You just can't hear it." We were both frustrated, because I felt I was doing a pretty good job at showing my appreciation, while at times she still felt unappreciated.

Then when I read *The Five Languages of Appreciation in the Workplace*, it was like someone had flicked on a switch in my dim head and everything looked bright again. I sheepishly realized that I'd been speaking "words of affirmation" as my love language (because that's one of my own primary languages) whenever trying to show Liv my appreciation. And when I bought her those presents, that was me speaking in the "tangible gifts" language. Neither of those languages are Liv's languages. I mean, sure, what person is going to say no to a bit of extra love in the form of a gift, but I was missing the mark and she wasn't feeling it.

Because I knew Liv well and was now armed with this new information, I was able to work out straightaway that her primary language is "quality time." In fact, it's the thing she'd ask of me the most, and because it's not my language, it's the one thing I'd try to avoid the most. Since having this epiphany, I've worked really hard to make sure I reach out and get enough one-on-ones in the calendar for us, and I'm trying, where I can, to carve out more time for her, even if it's just to have a brief conversation that starts with, "Tell me how things are going for you at the moment."

The language of quality time is not just about sitting next to someone all day—it's really about the quality of the time you spend together. People whose primary appreciation language is quality time might be grateful for you joining them as they head out to get their daily coffee or even accompanying them as they run an errand at lunchtime. It's more about giving them your personal attention, because this is when they feel loved and appreciated the most.

I remember a time when I employed a gorgeous girl, Samir, on my team. Samir was completely magnetic: her smile was infectious, and I never saw her sad. You couldn't help but giggle and feel a little more upbeat when Samir was around. She was a part-timer and only worked in my company two days a week, and those two days were often the highlights of my week. Thinking about Samir's time with us now, though, it's crystal clear to me that her appreciation language was appropriate physical touch. We were a small business back then of about fifteen people. Samir would bounce into the office on those two days—she always lifted the energy and nothing was ever a problem for her—but I soon learned that not everyone in the team felt the same about her enthusiasm for touch. The first thing Samir would do every day when she arrived at the office was to go around to every single person and give them a huge bear hug and a kiss on the cheek. At the time I thought it was brilliant—I mean, you can't make this stuff up! Samir was a true real-life fairy, and I'd never seen anything like it before. How lucky were we to have someone so delightful working with us?

The problem was that not everyone speaks in the language of "appropriate physical touch" and a few of my other team members just found it very uncomfortable and awkward. They staged an intervention of sorts and called a meeting with me. "Em, you have to stop her from doing this to us!" they said. "What do you mean, what has she done?" I asked them incredulously. "She comes in and hugs us every single day, and it's way too much!" they all said. I laughed and promised I'd talk to her, which I did, and Samir watered her hugs and kisses down to just a huge smile and wave from then on.

If you've been given the privilege of leading others, take a moment to think about their appreciation languages (this might take some discovery and discussion to find out), and do your best to speak in those languages wherever you can.

RULE #63: FANCY CHAIRS FOR EVERYONE

I'll never forget the day I received a direct message from a woman who'd seen me at the end of one of our huge events. It was late in the afternoon, the crowds had left, there were a handful of exhibitors left packing up their stands, and the cleaners were settling in for a long night ahead.

In one section of the event space, there were 500 rented chairs to be folded down and stacked up. I rolled up my sleeves and got to work. This woman caught me in the middle of the task, three chairs under each arm, laughing along with a few of my teammates. In her message, she wrote: "I'd spent the day listening to you speak up there on stage and was so impressed, but seeing you like that afterward (when no one was watching) took my breath away. Leaders can say whatever they want, but their actions speak so much louder than words, and I was so inspired that you were in there doing the work just as much as your team."

Reading this woman's happy message made me remember an unhappier story from a friend of mine, Molly. Molly worked at a medium-sized advertising agency for a number of years. As the business grew, so too did the environment: there were bigger offices, more meeting rooms, more people and more projects. She told me that she'd never forget the morning she walked in and saw two brand-new fancy ergonomic chairs there. Molly excitedly mentioned the chairs to her manager in passing and asked if their team would be getting them too. The manager wasn't sure but thought it was a great idea, so promised to ask on behalf of the team. Turns out the chairs were just for the two owners of the agency, and the request got declined. From then on, those two new chairs served as a reminder to Molly that the two owners mattered more than the rest of the team did.

I can't ask my team to do any job I wouldn't be willing to do myself, nor would I expect them to work under any conditions I wouldn't work under myself. I'm not above picking up the phone to chase a debtor or pitch to a client if I can be useful— and if I couldn't afford a fancy new chair for everybody, then I sure as hell wouldn't just get one for myself.

RULE #64: AGITATE TO BE BETTER

In so many of our meetings, I'll sit back and listen carefully to the debate and opinions being expressed around the table. It's easy to fall into the trap of groupthink where everyone goes along with the consensus of the group in an attempt to reach an outcome faster because, well, it's just easier. After all, everyone at that table has lots to get on with, and it's less painful (and quicker!) to go along with the majority sentiment. Being vulnerable and going against the grain takes courage, though. Being the one to say, "Hmm, I'm not sure. Are we missing something here?" is definitely the braver option.

Like with any business, we've experimented with our visual identity over the years. We've changed our logo, our colors and our tagline a few times as we've grown as a business and more deeply understood who we want to be. We're lucky to employ very skilled design people now who are passionate about the visual brand and do a wonderful job of managing it. But every now and then we lose our way and go off course. I'm often the last one to see any visual brand changes, with the team presenting the final result to me and not bothering me with all the iterations along the way. If I don't catch it early enough, though, I can be put in a difficult position. If I'm shown something that I don't like or that feels like too much of a departure from "us," the easiest thing would be for me to say, "Oh, it's great, well done." The more unpopular decision is to say, "We can do better," which often means going back to the drawing board and starting all over. Dang.

It's a strong leader's role to hold up a mirror to your people's greatness and gently encourage them forward until you know they've stretched and grown from it. Being a strong leader also at times means making the harder, more unpopular decision that needs to be made.

Amazing leaders don't have a need to make people feel comfortable when they sense that their discomfort may shift us all for the better. One of our members, Dixie Crawford, is incredible at this. As an Aboriginal woman, she's constantly agitating for growth when it comes to discussing race and privilege. She won't back down because someone is uncomfortable. Instead, she challenges people to see another perspective and equips them with new information so they can do their own work on exploring these vital issues.

To me, leadership in its rawest form is not being scared to seek and to question, and when we see people who have fallen asleep, we need to make it our responsibility to wake them up. More importantly, we need to be willing participants when it comes to others doing the same for us.

RULE #65: KILL THE GROUPTHINK

Brainstorming didn't unleash the potential of the group,
but rather made each individual less creative.

Jonah Lehrer

If there's one thing I'll do almost anything to avoid, it's group-think. As I said before, groupthink is basically when decisions are made as a group, robbing the process of creativity and ensuring no one in particular is truly responsible for the outcome.

In a lot of companies, individuals don't speak up and express their opinions, knowledge or expertise, because they don't want to rock the boat or make people feel uncomfortable. Or they're worried about having their ideas belittled or shot down. Their desire to maintain relationships and preserve harmony feels more important than disagreeing with the consensus. Instead, they stay silent, and that silence can be misinterpreted as agreement. This can lead to flawed decision-making, a lack of innovation, a loss of revenue and, if not picked up soon enough, the death of a business or effective team altogether.

It's something I've seen play out again and again by groups of well-intentioned teammates who don't want to offend anyone and want to make sure they keep the peace. They also don't want anyone to think they're less intelligent or their idea is a silly one, so they just nod and smile along with the group.

In the virtual/remote-working world, groupthink has increased. In fact, it's now got its own name: Zoomthink. It's awkward to speak up at times over a computer screen—there can be slight delays, and the tech can be glitchy. We also struggle to hear every word being spoken, and we lose the body language and other nuances that are easier to interpret when we're face-to-face. In most cases it's easier to just sit there and nod and smile.

The 1986 Space Shuttle Challenger disaster is known as one of the most significant cases of groupthink. It's widely reported that engineers and managers knew about potential problems with the launch, but because of "go fever" didn't speak up. The results were disastrous, with the spacecraft exploding 73 seconds into its journey and killing all seven crew members onboard.

Here are some ideas to combat groupthink if you're seeing it emerge in your workplace:

Zip it If you're the leader of the group, try sitting back and not contributing your opinion, at least not at first. Humans are wired to want to both impress and agree with the person who holds the most authority in the room, so instead of putting forward your ideas, listen to what others are saying and try not to influence the group by expressing yours.

Silence is golden Ask the team to take a few moments to collect their thoughts and write down their opinions, ideas and solutions. During this time no one is allowed to speak so that individual suggestions can be recorded.

Break up the team Form smaller groups and have them go away to problem-solve before returning to present to the broader group. This is a sure-fire way to increase diversity of thought, and the smaller the group, the better.

Work through each suggestion Instead of dismissing an idea, analyze it and discuss the pros and cons before coming to a conclusion.

Get outside help If you have an important decision to make and fear you might be at risk of groupthink, bring a consultant in to help manage the process to ensure you're not missing something.

If you find yourself in a problem-solving session and you've got a thought about something that could be done better, express it. Find your voice and put forward your opinion. If it lands aggressively, practice being gentler in your approach. Or practice speaking more assertively if you're usually one to hold back. And, if no one's listening, find a new audience or find a different way to deliver the message. Just don't do nothing and ignore the problem if it's yet to be solved. It's not just leaders who are responsible for seeing problems and finding better solutions—really, that's up to all of us.

own.

TWO

Half of my salary each week gets dropped at an amazing ice-cream store here in LA called Salt + Straw, because sometimes I struggle to know what to do with all these kids and ice cream is regularly the answer.

Salt + Straw sells the most incredible ice cream (I challenge you to go on their website right now and not immediately get a hankering for a scoop or two). Salt + Straw have become famous for lots of reasons: the quality of their ingredients is superior, their people are passionate about ice cream, and you can't even see the ice cream when you order, which is kind of a unique take on serving it up. More than anything, though, they're known for their wacky flavors. Ever thought of banana peanut butter tofu pudding? How about strawberry honey balsamic black pepper? Or pear and blue cheese? Me neither. Lucky they have lots of less adventurous options, and lucky I have so many kids, because that means I've pretty much tried all of them.

In the same way an ice cream containing blue cheese will not be everybody's choice, neither will you and your brand. Most companies spend their lives going after every single person and get despondent when they realize not everyone will buy. The smart operators home their intention on those they know they can serve best and who'll align the most with their values. It takes tremendous courage to stand out in front of your business or company and yell, "We're not for everyone!"

The same goes for your personal brand at work. One of the most liberating things you can learn in life is that not everyone has to like you, and that's okay. Too many of us have become people pleasers—constantly shape-shifting to suit everyone around us and burying our authentic selves. I've been guilty of this plenty of times! The thing is, when we build ourselves around others' expectations—from how we present ourselves to our passions, our personality and our behavior—then we lose the chance to celebrate what makes each of us unique and forge relationships with those who appreciate our real selves.

When the doors open at a Business Chicks event, we play the music loud. We've been known to ask members to stand up and dance and look silly at times; if you're a person who struggles with what people might think of you, then you're probably going to struggle in this moment too.

Once someone complained that we were "too generous," and another said we were "too polished." People have tried to tell us that we're "too pink" and that we should tone it down, but it's us and it's not for everyone. (The irony is that when you get past all this superficial stuff, you'll actually find a bunch of highly intelligent women working tirelessly to advance the game for other women at every turn. It's about the furthest from a hot pink dance party you could ever find, but that's the magic of brands that have a lot of depth, I suppose.)

Over the years we've had people come and experience Business Chicks and never return again because it's not for them. That's cool. Let me repeat for effect: you cannot please everyone.

If one thing has worked well for us, it's this: we've been clear about serving people who also want the salted malted chocolate chip cookie dough. Metaphorically, that's our flavor and they're our people. Those who are satisfied with vanilla can go elsewhere.

RULE #66: COMPETE WITH YOU

You can't look at the competition and say you're going
to do it better. You have to look at the competition
and say you're going to do it differently.

Steve Jobs

I have a girlfriend who makes amazing jewelery, and every time I see her and ask how business is, she complains about how others have stolen her ideas and that everyone is copying her. I'll always respond with, "Who cares? Stop worrying about it, and just keep being you." "But they copied our idea!" she'll cry. "They're doing everything the same as us!"

The first thing to do if you're worried about competitors is to lose your indignation a little. I love my friend with all my heart, but she did not invent cocktail rings or personalized bracelets. You too most likely did not invent the idea of skincare, or mortgage broker, or clothes, or jewelery or consulting or whatever it is you or your employer is trying to build.

Netflix didn't invent movies. Uber didn't invent cars. Amazon didn't invent warehousing and distribution. Most businesses start as a hybrid of something that already exists, hopefully executed way better and probably packaged and marketed better as well, almost always making life easier for the customer, no matter what they sell.

While we were early to the women's space and certainly have the advantage of being in the game for a long time, my business is easily copied. I actually like that it's easily copied as it keeps us innovating and trying to continually raise the bar. If competitors want to come in and do what we've done, they're completely entitled to! In the past couple of years, we've seen a huge rise in the number of women's communities, and the number of businesses and individuals running events and conferences just like ours.

I know there's going to be an element of them studying us and studying what has made Business Chicks work, but I also know this: the one thing people cannot ever copy is you.

You are your uniqueness, and you need to dial that up. We waste time when we sit and worry about what our competitors are or aren't doing. The time you spend lamenting about what others are up to will be much better spent focusing on how you can improve.

If you're a sole trader or a small business, it's easier to do this. It's easier to have your customers get to know you, fall in love with you, start to trust you and see you as a valuable partner in whatever journey it is they're on. We buy from those we trust, so spend your time investing in building that loyalty so that when they come to make choices about which skin-care product they're going to put on their face or which piece of jewelery they're going to buy, they choose you. Get good at storytelling, get good at being grateful with the customers you do have, get good at asking for referrals and then get good at rewarding those referrals.

Instead of shifting your focus externally, focus on what you can do better to create a really strong brand. That may mean spending time thinking about your point of difference (could your packaging be better, your customer experience stronger, your marketing message cleaner, your ambassadors more engaged? . . .). Get really clear on who's buying your products and services, and spend the time looking after them and finding more people like them.

This philosophy carries across to you and your personal career. Don't spend time worrying about your colleague's promotion or pay raise unless there is something clearly unfair that needs addressing. The point is, looking sideways only distracts you from moving forward. You do you.

RULE #67: YOU'RE ALLOWED TO CHANGE YOUR MIND

Zara McDonald and Michelle Andrews are two smart women who, over the past four years, have built one of the smartest companies I've seen in a long time—Shameless Media. Their business started off as a podcast—a side project the two created while working in junior media roles—and has grown to include multiple podcasts, content, lucrative sponsorships deals, book deals and speaking gigs. The pair now have five staff, and in the midst of the pandemic, they launched their first book—an instant bestseller called *The Space Between*.

I really enjoy following Zara and Michelle's journey, and I get a sense that they are not scared to make some tough decisions that might appear counterintuitive to what they're trying to build. In June 2020, the Shameless Facebook group was humming along and enjoyed strong engagement for the 39,000 members in there, but Zara and Michelle made the decision to close it down.

What I love about the way Zara and Michelle run their business is that they stand for something, even though their decisions might sometimes fly in the face of conventional wisdom and even if it means upsetting a few people along the way.

A few years back we started a program for entrepreneurs. These entrepreneurs had to apply to be part of the program, and there were strict criteria to join. Once successful, the business owners were placed into small groups, each from different industries. They'd meet up once a month with one of our trained facilitators to guide them through a framework that we had designed in consultation with peer-to-peer coaching experts in America. Not only was it a smart product—it gave these women the chance to connect and learn in a highly effective way and forged trust and deep friendship very quickly—it was also a profitable one. A couple of years into the program, though, I started to notice a culture of elitism and righteousness emerging, and it didn't feel like us at all. Then one day one of the entrepreneurs yelled at a team member of ours, and that was the same day I said, "Nope, stop. This is enough now." Entitled people who feel they're better than others will never be tolerated on my watch. My values are strong, and I will always stand for something more than just making money, so we made the decision to close the program.

Sometimes our fear of pissing people off keeps us suffering in situations we know we don't want to be in anymore. We copped a lot of criticism for changing our minds and removing the initiative, but deep down I knew it was the right thing to do.

RULE #68: STAND FOR SOMETHING

In the wake of the Parkland high school shooting in Florida in 2018 that killed seventeen students and injured another seventeen, activists pressured major retailers to stop selling assault-style rifles and high-capacity magazines. Calls like this have come and gone before, but this time an unexpected brand agreed. Dick's Sporting Goods said it would no longer sell the item, and would no longer sell firearms to anyone under the age of twenty-one. Hunting products make up about 10 percent of the company's sales, but CEO Edward Stack was willing to take the hit. "Following all the rules and laws, we sold a shotgun to the Parkland shooter in November 2017," he wrote in a letter explaining the decision. "It was not the gun he used in the shooting. But it could have been."

I believe that you can inspire others through the decisions you make and through the values you stand by despite it setting you back temporarily. For example, one of our team members recently said no to a deal with a brand that celebrated colonialism in their latest collection. Given that we are focused on and committed to our anti-racism work, that wasn't something we could get behind. It's inspiring to me that our team member knew to say no immediately and show leadership on this issue, when the brand she was working with thought it wasn't such a big deal. That brand wasn't happy with us for declining their offer, but I'd like to think our beliefs started a discussion for them internally in their business and they might think differently next year.

That old saying rings true here: if you don't stand for something, you'll fall for everything. Stand strong, friends.

RULE #69: DROWN OUT THE VOICE OF OTHERS

There have been a handful of times in my life when I have listened to other people's advice when deep down I knew I shouldn't.

When the opportunity to buy Business Chicks first came up, almost everyone around me told me not to buy it. At the time I had another business that was doing well. For many people, that business would have been enough—it was profitable, we had an awesome culture, we were doing really good work. I enjoyed it. It challenged me. And from the outside looking in, there was no real reason for me to try something new.

Still, I was resolute that buying this new company was the right thing for me to do. I couldn't think of anything else. I couldn't stop writing to-do lists in multiple notebooks all around my apartment filled with the ideas I had on how I was going to turn it into a huge success. I even kept a notebook by the shower, as that's when the inspiration seemed to hit. I'd call all my friends, and I'd talk about nothing else. I knew it was the right move for me, but everyone kept telling me I was stupid, and that I should just stick to what I was doing.

The more I listened to other people's opinions, the less sure I felt. And then I started doing what too many of us do. I started overthinking.

When I started to overthink, the doubt set in. In order to try to reassure myself, I hired a management consultant to do some due diligence. He looked at the financial statements and also my projections based on a new business model I had in mind. A few days later he delivered his findings: he told me that Business Chicks was not a business. That it made no money and was never going to make any money. He told me it made no sense to invest in it, and his advice (since I was asking for it) was to not move forward with the sale and to focus on the profitable business I already had.

At the time I'd also go to my sessions with that mentor I mentioned earlier, and he'd echo the opinion of the management consultant: "This girls thing you want to do . . . there's no money in that," and when I'd tell my friends what the management consultant and the mentor had said, a few of them also started to be less positive about the idea.

Still, something was telling me to go for it, so I listened to none of them.

I'm obviously really grateful that I didn't take anyone's advice and that I went forward with what my gut was feeling. I'm a massive believer that we should do what feels right, even when no one else is feeling the same.

RULE #70: REMEMBER
YOU'RE NEVER TOO SMALL

I said somebody should do something about that.
And then I realized I was somebody.

Lily Tomlin

Perhaps the greatest gift of working remotely is the space it gives us to see things in perspective. I have an added bonus in that the majority of my people are working in another time zone, so that when I wake up, they're still sleeping. I'm given the luxury to think expansively without my inbox pinging every two minutes and having to be on endless conference calls. The space frees me up for a good few hours to think about how we're faring as a company and how we could improve.

Each week I video dial-in to our big company-wide meeting and see the team sitting there. A few months back I started to feel frustrated with how many disposable coffee cups I was seeing. I was frustrated because I knew we had a kitchen full of reusable cups, and I also knew we could do better. The other frustrating thing was that we'd already asked them to please use their reusable cups, but we still weren't really getting there.

I decided to take a hard line on the issue, writing this email to the team:

Hey team,

About a month back I decided that I wanted to make our headquarters a disposable coffee cup-free office. I know we asked for your help with this, but on the team meeting the other day I noticed we'd slipped back a little.

A quick Google search tells me more than fifty billion coffee cups are thrown out every year in the US. *Fifty billion!* This makes me feel sick. Now our little office may represent the tiniest drop in the ocean, but hopefully our leadership can inspire other offices to do the same?

I reckon we can do this. We can commit to making us completely disposable cup-free. It's going to take some changing of habits and a bit of awkwardness/work, but we're all super smart and we can figure it out.

Can I suggest that (as a start) we just make a rule that says there are no disposable coffee cups allowed in the office? This means that if you slip up and order one on your way to work, it's not allowed to be brought into the office. Now of course this isn't a solution (because the coffee has been already bought), but it'll help us retrain our brains out of the habit. If you see someone come into the office with one, make a joke and tell them they have to stand outside with it (for reals!). I know this sounds ridiculous, but we'll all learn super quickly this way! And when someone gets up to go get a coffee from downstairs, remind them to grab a mug from the kitchen.

We could also take it a step further—when we're confirming meetings at our office, you could email the person and say something like, "Just to let you know that while we love our caffeine, we're proudly a disposable cup-free office, so please don't bring them into our space. We'll happily go grab you a coffee at any time, but we'll be using a mug to keep one more paper cup from being used and discarded." I think people will actually respect us for showing leadership on this. If you don't stand for something, you'll fall for everything, right?

If it'd help, I'm happy to buy anyone who needs it a reusable cup, and maybe (if you're already in the habit of doing this) you can throw it in your bag every day so it's there to order your coffee with the next morning?

I don't want anyone to feel guilty or bad about this. We have to start where we are, and there should be no shame in that. But let's just work together to make a small difference!

Thanks so much,

Em

Of course, everyone was on board philosophically, but there was a little bit of back-and-forth on whether we should relax our stance a little. One well-meaning team member responded and said, "Maybe we could start a charity jar, and if you bring in your disposable cup one day by mistake, then you have to put a gold coin in the jar?" I loved her initiative and respected the thinking, but still felt strongly that we had to make this a rule and not a "we hope you do this" type of situation.

And when it comes to the environment, we actually don't have the wiggle room we'd all like to be halfhearted on this. We need leaders who are going to make strong, bold statements and find solutions rather than be polite and suggestive. If we're not going to lead, then who is?

I'm told that after the email was received, the policy was pretty much implemented immediately. Our culture is strong and our people care a lot about the bigger picture (including the environment), so it wasn't too much of a leap to make.

We were proud to eliminate this waste from our office, but the story gets a little more exciting as other people in our community started to join in too.

One of our members decided to take on the challenge for the company she works for as well. She excitedly messaged us to say she was on board, and then a few weeks passed before the next email arrived with a "Hooray, I did it!" This member explained how she had worked hard to get the buy-in from the powers that be and how it only took a few short weeks to announce their plan in a company-wide memo. They set a date for the change to take place, consulted with the on-site café downstairs as to their plan, put posters up all around their sites, and the result is that 42,000 disposable cups are now not heading into landfill each year.

It's also a beautiful lesson in personal leadership for that woman and one that she'll carry with her for the rest of her career.

RULE #71: START WITH ONE

Whenever I give speeches or write about the initiatives we're trying to make happen in our business, people often say, "I tried, but the leaders in my company won't do anything about it."

My answer to them is that you have to start and lead where you can. Tag—you're it! You're the leader! Influence what you can. Start with one! One person, one idea, one decision. And that advice stands whether you are trying to influence your colleagues to work smarter or influence your manager to give you more responsibility. If you've got a dream or a goal, it's about somehow finding the confidence to take that first step and get on your way. What's that quote about not needing to see the whole staircase? It's true—it's all about taking one step at a time and keeping on climbing up no matter what.

If you can't get the whole company to change, can you get one colleague to? If you're struggling to get yourself out of debt, could you start by cutting up a credit card or two or setting up a direct debit of just $20 a month into a high interest–bearing account? If you're unfit, could you get out this afternoon for ten minutes and take a walk around the block?

Maybe it's getting an email out. Or making a phone call. Perhaps it's having a conversation you know you need to have. What's the one thing you can do now to push you that little bit closer to whatever it is you really want?

act.

You don't have to own a company or manage budgets and run a team of people to be a leader. Leadership is within all of us. I think we can all agree on that philosophically—that we can all be leaders—but the problem is that lots of people forget this, choosing for their fallback to be criticism and complaint. In some ways it's easier to criticize the people "above" us and to complain about the way things are, instead of taking a deep breath and saying, "Okay, this is the situation—what can I do to influence it? How can my great attitude and my ideas and my support play a part in making things better?'

In my mind, the best leaders (whether they have the title or not) are people who consistently show a bias for action and positivity. Instead of stopping their exploration with a negative attitude—"This is too hard," "I'd never know how to do that," "I don't have the time for that," "I don't have the answers"—they continue their discovery and instead get fixated on how it might be possible to make improvements and to make them now.

RULE #72: RADICAL ACTION

One of my favorite movies of all time is *The Pursuit of Happyness*. The main character, Chris Gardner, is played by actor Will Smith. The film is based on Gardner's life, and his story is the best example of radical action ever. He's a father who falls on hard times after a failed business venture. His marriage breaks down, and he's left to fend for himself and his young son. Gardner ends up applying for an internship at a brokerage firm and is one of twenty people to be given the opportunity. The unpaid internship lasts for six months, and they're told only one person out of the twenty will get a paid role at the end. Even though Gardner is homeless throughout this time, he still gives his all, sometimes sleeping in bathrooms at train stations, sometimes in churches. The story goes on to have a happy ending: Gardner is the last man standing and gets the paid job, eventually going on to create his own firm and become a very wealthy man.

Aerial skier Alisa Camplin also has an incredible story of radical action. Alisa had a goal from a young age to represent her country at the Olympics. She had no idea which sport would get her there, eventually deciding on aerial skiing, even though she'd never actually seen snow at the time she made that decision. Her next goal was to get to the 2002 Salt Lake City Olympics. Not being able to secure sponsorship, Alisa had to pay for all of her own training (and aerial skiing is not a cheap sport). Alisa worked a nine-to-five job as a senior executive with IBM, and at night she alternated between delivering pizza and teaching gymnastics to schoolchildren. On the weekends she didn't stop either—she cleaned houses. "It was a real struggle, but I did it the hard way," Alisa said. How she actually found time to train is beyond me, but that's what radical action is: an extraordinary person exhibiting extraordinary efforts to achieve their goal. Remarkably, Alisa's radical action paid off. She won the gold medal (even though she broke both ankles in a training accident a few weeks before the Olympics). Alisa Camplin has a mind of steel and a focus like no one else I've ever met.

My ex-husband and I have my own story of radical action. We got desperate when we first moved to the United States. We had four kids at the time and had just left the comforts of our home country, where we'd worked hard to set ourselves up, living in a comfortable neighborhood with great schools. I ran a successful business and we were growing, and there was no real reason, apart from ambition and opportunity, that we had to move.

We emigrated to Los Angeles, bought a house, filled it with things and pretty promptly ran out of money. Being new to the country and having no credit rating meant that the interest rate on our loan was unreasonably high, and we were probably unreasonably optimistic about how quickly we could scale up, too, which is never a good combo. I'd set aside a budget to move and establish my business in America, and once that was gone, I was staring at a nil bank balance and wondering what to do with this new house and all our things (and the many children living inside of it).

Enter radical action. We needed a solution, and we needed it fast, so we got a photographer in, popped the photos up on Airbnb, and voila, we were on our way to making (some) money. We quickly worked out that we could rent out our four-bedroom house, and whenever we got a booking, we'd go and rent a two-bedroom place.

It was not easy money. Imagine packing up a large family and moving them every time a booking came in—we did it, dammit. Every weekend. We had to. All those dresses, toys, tubes of toothpaste, family photos . . . We turned it into one big adventure and we got it done. Sometimes there would be a few of us in each bed, someone on the couch, and of course there were times when the baby's cot was set up in the bathroom.

When I look back now, I'm proud of us. The "adventure" was completely disruptive and thankfully short-lived (if you call a year short-lived). Would we ever do it again? Absolutely. This radical action got us through a really tricky time and taught me a lot. It taught me about what I didn't want and what I didn't need, and the suffering and effort shaped me in ways that success was never quite able to. If we hadn't taken these steps, I guess we would have had to move back to Australia with our tails between our legs, which wouldn't have killed us, but it wasn't our goal.

During our intense Airbnb survival tactics, an opportunity to rent a much cheaper home came up, and we jumped at it. It was a little more inconvenient—a further commute to the kids' schools, and the airport and so on—but the point is this: we learned we can do almost anything for the short term, and the radical action of saying yes to this downgrade allowed us to build the home we're now in.

I have a girlfriend who's thirty-two and was desperate to get into the property market and buy an apartment. She looked at her situation, consulted a financial planner, did her research, crunched her numbers and worked out that it wasn't going to happen at her current rate. For like ten years or so. That time-frame was unacceptable to her, so instead of resigning herself to accept it, she moved into radical action. She gave up the room in the apartment she was renting at $370 per week and moved back in with her parents. She cut up two credit cards and sold her car. She sold clothes on eBay. She stopped buying cocktails, opting for house wine instead, and she got more conscious of her spending. She spoke with her employer and came up with a plan to give them more output (designing a profitable product that they didn't yet offer), and asked for a pay raise if the product worked out. An agreement was struck that if she could get this product to market and make it a success, her employer would give her the pay raise she was asking for. After eight months, she's now sitting on a deposit of $60,000, has secured finance and is currently scouring the market for a place she can call her own.

I recently heard a very similar story from one of our young members, a twenty-six-year-old woman, named Eloise Abraham who wrote, "Christmas 2018 I received *Winging It*, devoured it in two days and signed up to become a Business Chicks member immediately. I took every sentence to heart and put it into practice, elevating myself in my 9–5 job and taking up a side hustle. I went to 9 to Thrive Summit (the Business Chicks one-day conference), and the fire inside of me further ignited me to smash all my goals. This weekend, after seven months of hard work, I put the sold sticker on my dream property in my dream suburb."

Most people don't really want to take radical action. It can be utterly exhausting. It takes effort. It takes persistence and willpower and smarts and sacrifice. It means having hard conversations, and it means going up against people who won't always understand your drive. But it works, and with a good reframe ("This is exhilarating!" "I'm getting there!" "I'm actually doing this!") it starts to become really, really fun.

You can use radical action for whatever your goal. I'm always going to encourage you to look beyond short-termism (that holiday you want next year) and instead aim for something that your future self will benefit from (property like Eloise, for example).

I ache to see more radical action. I live for it. The world would be such a better place if we had half the commitment of Chris Gardner or a quarter of the determination of Alisa Camplin. Instead, we settle. We lose time. We survive on autopilot. We talk ourselves out of opportunities and convince ourselves we don't have what it takes. Close your eyes for a moment and think about what you really want. What's that one thing you'd strive for if you knew there was no chance you could fail at it?

If you're struggling with your work-life balance and kids are part of that equation, your radical action could be to bring an au pair into your lives. This was life-changing for our family (even though I resisted for a while there), and now I couldn't live without that extra pair of hands around. It could be negotiating one day off a week with your employer, or it could mean, gasp, quitting that job and going elsewhere.

If you're not getting the support you need from your partner, the radical action could be to leave. You're allowed to. You have one life, and your purpose is not to stay unhappy and unfulfilled. If you're single and wanting to meet someone, your radical action could be to go on fifty dates in the next three months. Radical, I know, but life can sometimes be a game of chance, and the more you play it, the luckier you get.

If you're under financial pressure or have a big financial goal to achieve, consider renting out a room in your house to a student. Or taking on a second job. Or starting a little business on the weekends—friends of mine rent out jumping castles and popcorn machines as their side hustle, and another friend clears an extra $1,000 a week with a weekend market stall. Your radical action might look like buying bunk beds and sharing a room with a friend, halving your rent. You could stop buying new clothes (we all have enough, you know) or finally work out how to get organized to bring your own food into work each day.

Radical action in your workplace might be about letting some people go. I met a lady named Roula, who told me about the charity she'd started a decade ago. They did great work and made a difference, but Roula was completely worn down. What wore her down more than anything was not the consistent fundraising required to keep the charity alive or the hard work needed to fuel their efforts. No, what wore her down was the internal politics and constant bickering that came from within her team. They feuded endlessly, with two staff members having not spoken to each other for the best part of a year. It was exhausting for Roula. She'd tried everything within her power to resolve the internal culture dynamic, but nothing would budge. Roula told me how she simply woke up one day with a resolve to change. Something in her had shifted, and she now knew what was required. She walked into the office that day, and one by one fired every one of her four employees. Roula told me it was traumatic for all of them at the time, and two of them don't speak to her at all anymore, but her radical action transformed her life and the future trajectory of her organization. Roula went on to hire a brand-new team, and her mojo for what she does is well and truly back.

Similarly, I have a friend who leads a small team and is constantly complaining about her workload and stress levels. Looking in, I can see that her radical action right now would be to let one or two people go from that team, replacing them with better performers. That would free up her workload, reduce her stress and make her role more enjoyable. Will she be willing to take this radical action? Time will tell, but unfortunately the need to be liked and not rock the boat sometimes means we all miss out on a better way of being.

The real question is, how far are you willing to go to achieve your goals and get the job done? Business Chicks member Amanda Stevens told me her beautiful story of radical action.

It was early December 2019, and I was flying from Queenstown to Sydney, via Melbourne, for my hundred and fifth keynote presentation for the year. I was suffering from physical and emotional burnout.

Landing into Melbourne at about 7 p.m., I got a text message from the airline advising that my connecting flight to Sydney had been canceled due to smoke and that I was rebooked on a flight the next day which would have me land into Sydney at midday. I was due on stage for five hundred people at 9:30 a.m., so that wasn't going to work. My assistant was madly trying to grab flights, but they were disappearing as fast as she could book them.

I rang my driver, Yilmaz, who's been my driver for sixteen years, and asked him if he was up for a road trip to Sydney.

"Um, when?," he said.

"Um, now," I said.

Thirty minutes later he arrived at Melbourne Airport to pick me up with a pillow, a blanket and a packet of Tim Tams. He drove me through the night to Sydney. We arrived at 6 a.m., I got a couple of hours sleep and was on stage at 9:30 a.m.

I was probably overcompensating for being tired, because I believe it was my best presentation of the year, and I got a standing ovation.

So there you have it, my friends. Getting into radical action could just earn you a standing ovation or two. Go get it.

RULE #73: STOP MAKING EXCUSES

We've all got something, whether it's conscious or subconscious, holding us back.

It could be that you believe you're not smart enough. Perhaps it's that you think you don't have the right skills. Maybe deep down there's a sense that you don't deserve success. It's different for all of us.

Uncovering self-limiting beliefs is hard but powerful. As challenging as it is, I've always found it useful to talk with someone about the stories I'm telling myself and the excuses I'm using that are holding me back. Through this work, I've recognized that if I can name the belief, then I'm on my way to clearing it.

Here are the excuses I hear people use the most (and that I've been guilty of voicing from time to time too).

I don't have enough time You have the same number of hours in your day as Michelle Obama. You can choose how you spend your time. You have the right to say no to things that are taking up your time. You have the right to claw back your time by asking for help. You have the right to work with other people who can give you some time back, and you have the right to give up tasks that don't fulfill you.

I'm scared Fear is real, and it's debilitating. Dale Carnegie once famously said, "If you want to conquer fear, do not sit at home and think about it. Go out and get busy."

I'm not ready yet You and me both. You're never really ready.

I don't know how to start I didn't either. So I just started. While very few of us ever know the exact path we have to walk to reach our goals, we can all think of one small action we can take now to get going. Just one. Make a phone call. Book a coffee in with someone who might be able to help. Research something. Write down your idea or vision. Open a bank account. Buy a new pen and notepad. Anything, just start!

I don't have enough money Yeah, that old chestnut. Very few of us, the trust fund babies excluded, start out with a limitless checkbook. The good news is that money is relatively easy to come by these days. There are ways to get money, keep money and grow money. Go spend some time investing in yourself on how to do that. Get creative. Ask lots of questions. Do without something you're spending money on now. Read. Educate yourself.

It's not the right time When I first offered the chief executive officer role to Olivia Ruello, she hesitated. She told me it wasn't the right time. One of the excuses she used was that she was trying to get pregnant. I told her there would never be a right time to start a big new role, and there'd never be the right time to start a family either. If she wanted both of these things, she'd just have to walk toward them. Standing still wasn't going to get her there. Of course, Liv took the role and is excelling at it. She's also now excelling at parenting her four-year-old daughter and eight-month-old son.

This excuse really interests me, because I think at some level we all know that life doesn't work in some perfect order where the gates suddenly open and you're met with more money or more time to do the things you actually want to do. We all get that, yet we hide behind this excuse the most.

I'm not confident enough I get it. Very few people are born with the self-confidence of Kanye West. Generally, you'll find that most people who have a lot of self-confidence have worked really hard on it. I know I have. There have been many periods in my life where I've struggled with confidence and have experienced imposter syndrome, and it can be crippling. I've found the only answer to overcoming a lack of self-confidence is to put yourself continuously in situations that scare the heck out of you. That's how I did it, anyway. Saying yes to giving speeches in places where I felt like the most unaccomplished person in the room. Speaking up in meetings where it felt like I was the only one who didn't know the answers. Leaving relationships even though I didn't know where I'd go next. You only get confident through practicing doing the things that scare you until they don't.

I don't have enough experience Everyone started with no experience, and anyway, experience can often be prohibitive. Being naïve can be a beautiful thing, and it helps you become curious about attacking problems in ways that haven't been thought of before. Don't buy into this excuse, and don't let others curb your enthusiasm (unless you're a neurosurgeon, and in this case, I'd love it if you'd go get quite a few years of experience under your belt, thanks).

It's just too difficult Most great things in life present some complexity and difficulty. Love is complex and difficult, and yet we keep searching and longing for it. Traveling with toddlers is difficult, and yet we persist because the adventures we experience outweigh the short-term pain of dealing with a person on a plane who hates children and can't understand why they're there.

I'm afraid of what others might think I've always found this to be a comforting thought: mostly, people are so caught up in their own worries that they're not thinking very much about you. Also, once you get clear on the fact that you can't control what people think of you, you'll stop obsessing about it. It's completely natural to want to be liked, accepted and thought highly of. That's human nature, and it plagues us all. It's also completely natural for you to want to strive to be the best version of yourself, and if you're paralyzed thinking about what others think of you, then you're not going anywhere fast. Living your life according to the rules and expectations of others who you feel are judging you at any given turn is a fast way of not truly living.

Perhaps it's time to take a hard look at the people in your life and decide whether they're really supporting your growth? Surrounding yourself with positive people who believe in you and will back your dreams no matter what will surely lessen the amount of time you spend worrying about what others think. If this is a problem for you, then go talk with someone about it—getting clear on your motivations and self-limiting beliefs with a therapist or someone else you trust might help shift this one out of your way.

I might fail At some stage, you probably will. Oprah Winfrey was once fired for being too "emotionally invested in her stories." Louisa May Alcott was told to stick to her teaching and not bother writing, and Walt Disney was fired from a newspaper, being told he lacked creativity. Milton Hershey started three candy companies before going on to found the Hershey's chocolate empire, and I bet if I gave you ten minutes on Google you'd be able to find dozens more. We cannot let the idea of failing get in the way of starting, but so many people do.

RULE #74: HOPE IS NOT A STRATEGY

I want to share what went down in our company when the pandemic hit. A good chunk of our business is large-scale in-person events, so when the world came to a halt, I knew we were screwed. I had no idea how long we'd be screwed for, of course, but it was undeniable: we were screwed.

The first thing I did was get together a group of advisors—some from inside the business and some external people who knew me well and knew I'd be losing a lot of sleep at this stage. The first thing I said to them was this: "Give it to me straight. How many months of cash do we have left?" We played out several scenarios in these first few sessions, but whichever way you sliced and diced it, I knew we had to do something, and I knew we had to do it quickly. Two words kept repeating over and over in my mind about what we needed to do to survive this time: urgent action, urgent action, urgent action. Hope was not a strategy.

During these first few weeks, I was running on a few different tracks. One was a cost-saving track, and we were running fast. We sat down and interrogated every single line item on our profit and loss statement and made difficult decisions quickly. Some were easier to make—we'd have to downgrade our printer plan, for example, which made sense as no one was in the office anyway—and some were much, much harder—as I mentioned before, we couldn't afford to keep some of the people who were hired to create the experiences we could no longer deliver.

Knowing cost-cutting alone wouldn't be enough to save the business, I was also running on a revenue-making track. I was trying to mobilize everyone in the team to come up with ways we could turn our skills and expertise into something that we could actually sell and make meaningful for our amazing members and customers. Again, speed was important here. We had to be seen as leaders in this space, and we had to do it quickly.

The team rallied, and I was so proud of how they were able to get a massive online event together with an incredible line-up of international speakers in just a few days. We called that event AllStars, and it was a combination of some of the best speakers we'd heard from in the fifteen years of Business Chicks' history. We gave ourselves a week to sell that event, calling on every person we knew to buy a ticket.

From a dollars perspective, that event meant we were able to keep the business running for a few more weeks. And when that event proved successful, we rallied and did it again with an entirely new set of speakers; from there we just kept trying to keep things fresh with other digital offerings and brand extensions.

I'll always be grateful for all those speakers who shared their wisdom and all the people who bought a ticket and jumped online to support us. During this time, I was unshakable in my resoluteness about what we were trying to do. I needed to ensure the security and future of our business, because I knew exactly why we existed and why we held a place in the lives and hearts of our customers and our team.

When we were in the depths of the pandemic, our "why" was something I kept returning to time and time again. During those fifteen-hour days, our why, our reason for being, had never before appeared with such clarity. We're here to make the journey easier and more fulfilling for others. We're here to provide a space for people to come together and support one another and to continue the learning and the growing, and most importantly, we're here to help everyone feel a sense of possibility: that there *is* a light at the end of tunnel, that we can get through this and that we are going to do it together.

We shouldn't need a pandemic to teach us these lessons. If there's one thing I'm always talking about with my team (and my family), it's that hope is not a strategy and we can't wait for opportunities to fall from the sky and drop in our laps. I mean, there's luck and there's divinity, and all that can conspire to create cool shit from time to time, but for the most part, if we want to make magic happen, we've got to do that ourselves. It's a lesson in being proactive and not just mindlessly going through the motions, thinking that our past hard work will manifest in future similar results. For my kids, that might mean working a little harder on their chores so they can save for our next holiday, and for my colleagues and my team at work, it means getting out there and making stuff happen.

At times I'm sure I'm exhausting to the people around me, but I've never been one to sit back and say, "Hopefully next year is going to be a good year." No way. There's no hope. I believe in plotting and scheming to create opportunities so I can live intentionally and with purpose.

So, how do you create opportunities? I think it starts with thinking like an entrepreneur, no matter what your actual role is. Entrepreneurship isn't a career choice. It's a way of thinking. It's about getting into action. It's knowing the ideas won't manifest by themselves, and you have to take some responsibility for dreaming them up.

Almost fifteen months later, as I write this chapter, we're still not completely back to business-as-usual, nor can I imagine we will be for a long time. That said, my business is still standing, and I'm proud of the way we handled ourselves. We've grown as leaders, and we've taken the lessons learned through the pandemic and turned them into other opportunities. I'm now grateful for the fifteen-hour days and the nights where I only managed a bag of corn chips for dinner.

After all, we didn't just hope, we did.

grow.

You know what used to trip me up all the time? My beliefs about how things should be. "I'm this age, and by this age I really thought that I'd be here by now." Or "I've been working at this business for a decade, and I thought I'd be way more successful than I actually am."

My very wise coach does a great job at pulling out the best analogies when I need them most. During one of our more intense conversations, she had me think about how plants grow. She asked, "Does a gardener go outside and plant a seed and expect to come out the next day to find a huge lush plant providing shade for her? Does she look at it expectantly and say, 'Have you grown yet?'" Without waiting for an answer from me, my coach said: "She does not. The gardener first goes to her garden and decides where her plant will go. She tills the soil, then carefully plants the seed, and over many months of attention and nourishment, she waters that seed and its soil each day. The seed begins to sprout, the first sign of life emerges and finally she starts to feel that her efforts have been worth it. One day, many months later, it dawns on the gardener just how much her plant has grown. She takes a moment and marvels at how far it's come from that very first day when she decided where to plant it."

About halfway through this beautiful story, I could see where my coach was going. I'm no dummy. She was trying to get through to me that growth takes time. That humans are just like plants. That we need to water and nourish ourselves over and over again, and that—most importantly—we must be patient. I'm not wired to be particularly patient. I like my plants to grow quickly, thanks very much. I like deals to happen at lightning speed. I like people to action things pretty much as soon as I ask for them—just as I would in return.

There's definitely a time and a place for speed, but when it comes to growth, that work is muddy and slow and needs your endurance.

RULE #75: YOU'RE EXACTLY WHERE YOU'RE MEANT TO BE

I've always found a lot of comfort in thinking, "You're exactly where you're meant to be," and I've committed that mantra to heart, often falling back on it whenever I'm disappointed about an outcome. When you lift your thinking to become a little more patient and philosophical about the timing of your life, suddenly difficult situations appear far less challenging.

We've all heard countless stories of people who have lost their jobs or been forced to close or dramatically change their businesses in the last eighteen months, and for many of those people, the forced changes actually turned out to be the nudge they needed to change what wasn't working. I recently met Yvonne, a former long-haul flight attendant who lost her job when her airline employer was grounded. After initially being devastated at losing her role after twenty years of service, Yvonne sprang into action and got a job selling cars. Today, she says the change was exactly what she needed. She has a steady job that pays a little more, she no longer has to wake to a 4 a.m. alarm, and she sees her kids more than she has in years.

Business Chicks member Steph Prem will also tell you that sometimes, forced change is for the better. She calls it "divine timing." Steph is a former Winter Olympian who owns and runs Pilates studios. Overnight, Steph went from running three booming studios and managing sixteen staff to having to reimagine her entire business. Truth be told, however, it was the change she needed.

"The first lockdown essentially forced me to fast-track parts of my business I would not have looked at when I was working sixty-hour weeks and running (literally running haggard) between three studios. The time I was gifted became an opportunity to put back into other areas of the business and think more laterally about how else I could work more effectively and reach more people."

Eighteen months later—and after nine months of forced business closures—Steph's large headquarters and studio no longer exists, and she says she's better for it. She now services thousands more clients than she did before, via fewer studios, online programs, speaking engagements and delivering corporate wellness programs. Bricks and mortar, she says, is not the only way to reach and connect with people.

"As a former Olympian and Type A personality, I have the tendency to be very hard on myself. I believe in doing the work and fighting the good fight and not only surviving as a small business owner but thriving even in times of adversity. But it's a fine line, and as someone who preaches health, balance and equilibrium in life, I was not going to be good to anyone if I continued down the road I was on."

RULE #76: LET LIFE SURPRISE YOU

I'm making space for the unknown future
to fill up my life with yet-to-come surprises.

Elizabeth Gilbert

Six years ago, I packed up my family and moved them from Australia to Los Angeles so I could launch Business Chicks into North America. The first year of our relocation was a write-off. All I remember of those first twelve months is being in the depths of start-up despair, sacrificing everything—sleep, money, time with my family, my health—in order to survive. After I'd opened an office in New York, hired a bunch of people, bought a home, set up the company properly and navigated all the regulations required of companies launching in the US, I'd completely depleted our cash reserves, which is a fancy way of saying I had no money left. I didn't have any sort of safety net to speak of. My husband wasn't working at the time, and once I ran out of funds the Australian business had provided me with for the expansion, I was left scratching my head as to what my next move would be.

I could have started fundraising, but I was so exhausted that I knew I'd be lying to any investor who naturally requires their founder to be all-in. I couldn't look anyone in the eye and say I was ready to give my all. I'd started with my all, and somewhere along the way I had well and truly lost it.

During this time—without a doubt the hardest period of my career and my life so far—I looked down the barrel of failure and exhaustion, but I didn't entirely bury myself. Yes, I stayed home a lot and wasn't motivated to meet new people or do anything that required any extra energy from me. I just managed to find enough energy to face each day and do the bare minimum of what's asked of a parent to four kids at the time and of the owner of a company whose idea hasn't gone according to plan. You could say I was hibernating, waiting for sunnier days, but really, I was just well and truly stuck.

I had enough foresight to seek support during this time. I hired that very wise coach I just mentioned (who I still work with today), and I'm not sure she understood much of what I was saying during our first session over Skype—I cried many tears of shame and wiped my nose so many times that I gave Rudolph the reindeer a run for his money. The sessions got easier, as they always do, and over time she helped me see that it's impossible to keep moving at full throttle without having some of the wheels fall off. She helped me see that it's okay not to keep climbing as aggressively as I had been, and that it's okay to pause for a while and regroup. I came to refer to this period of my life as base camp. I'd been climbing the mountain of entrepreneurship for so many years and had reached a fairly high cliff on the edge of that mountain, but now my body was telling me, "Stop, go no further. Rest here. Acclimate." So metaphorically I built a tent, rolled out a sleeping bag and lay on the side of that mountain while I took time to catch my breath from the past twenty years of building companies and the more recent failure of trying to start one.

You might see a little of yourself in this story? I think burnout and not being able to know which way to turn is becoming more common for us all, and it can be confusing and debilitating. We're often so wound up about how the world will perceive us that we lose the ability to tune into what we really want from our lives. From this experience of resting at base camp for a while, I now know that the best view comes after the hardest climb.

If I hadn't taken this time out to properly grieve the failure I'd experienced and give myself the space to think and create, many things wouldn't be out in the world—during this time I secured my first book deal and went on to write *Winging It*; I developed a brand-new product with our international Knowledge + Study Tours, which have garnered a cult following; and our fifth child, Piper (who's such a delight), was also born.

What those years generously taught me (and it's a lesson we all need to hear from time to time) is this: don't be in such a rush to figure everything out. Rest a little at base camp if that's what's required. Get good at embracing the unknown, and let your life surprise you.

RULE #77: YOU ONLY NEED ONE YES

Arianna Huffington got rejected by 36 publishers when she pitched her second book. When I first heard those numbers, I didn't really believe them, thinking surely they must be a little bit embellished for the sake of a good story. At the time I couldn't understand how anyone could recover from being rejected all those times without feeling like they were a huge loser. And then the exact same thing happened to me.

The initial publishing deal for my first book was just for Australia and New Zealand, so we started shopping around the rights for America, thinking it'd be as easy breezy as it had been the first time around. And with that naïve assumption, so began the universe's cruel game of ensuring I suffered in the same way Arianna had.

For months, I pounded the New York pavements in the snow, schmoozing every publisher who'd take a meeting with me. One met me at a Starbucks in the Financial District, telling me she'd be sure to pitch it in. Never heard from her again. One guy took the matcha latte I bought him at a café in Midtown, promising the world, before disappearing into the cold New York winter, never to be seen again. At one particularly harsh meeting, they didn't even save me the embarrassment of holding their rejection over for an email the next day, instead announcing, "It's not for us," right then and there, followed by awkward silence as I gathered my coat and beanie and got the hell out of there. That meeting sent me straight to a downtown bar where I ordered a shot of vodka before steeling myself for the next showdown. I'll admit that was a low point.

My book agent was working overtime to ensure we got the job done, and her next move was to line up a meeting with a publisher out of San Francisco. She called me and said, "These guys want to meet you in person, and there'll be at least five of them in the meeting. You don't happen to be in San Francisco at all in the next week, do you?" I told her, as luck would have it, I would indeed be there next Tuesday and Wednesday. As soon as I hung up from that call with my agent, I booked my flights.

The following Wednesday morning, I showed up on that publisher's doorstep. I knew this was the one, and they acted as if they knew it too. My agent dialed in from New York for the meeting and when it was over I called her from an Uber on the way back to the airport. We all but said, "We did it!" because every cue the publisher gave was that they were all in.

The acquiring editor of that publishing house showed an unreasonable level of enthusiasm and kept my hopes high for days, even sending me a gift with a handwritten note: "Can't wait to be your American publisher!" Still, something was up, because where was my deal? Five days passed after our first meeting, and then came a confusing call saying, "We absolutely love you but can't publish you," with no real further explanation. Dang (and pass another shot of vodka, please).

The rejections continued to flow. One publisher ushered me into her dingy office and had to move a stack of books from a chair so I could sit. I couldn't see one inch of her mahogany desk as it was covered several feet high with piles of paper and books. She said, after it had become clear she had no interest in me, "Yeah, maybe you need to get a podcast first." I wanted to say, "Yeah, maybe you need to clean your desk first," but of course I didn't. There were the two senior executives at a publishing house who told me, "You're great, but the category is crowded." Another said, "You need more of a platform." Another said, "You have something special, but you are unproven. Come back when you have three books under your belt." Another: "Tell me how many Australians you've ever heard of on the *New York Times* bestseller list?" And so it went on.

It was so soul-destroying that I told my agent not to tell me about the responses anymore. I was in a deep relationship with defeat that was best explored alone rather than fueled by any more rejection.

Still, my long-suffering agent had a job to do, and one day she called to reason with me. "Okay Em, we've exhausted pretty much every single publisher in the land, so I think it's time to have a conversation about where we go next. I do, however, have three publishers that still have the book in front of them, and one would like to have a call with you tomorrow."

I took the call reluctantly with that publisher, expecting my ego was in for a final blow, but I put my big girl pants on and showed up like the pro I am.

The call started in the same way a lot of calls with publishers had started: they say all the right things and you begin to think you have a chance. I wouldn't let myself get too excited, but I had to admit this one felt a little different, like a good Tinder date out of another hundred that hadn't worked out. I didn't need to do much talking, as the publisher was happy to share how much she'd loved reading the book (a friend had brought it to her in New York when she'd visited from Australia), and how when the pitch had crossed her desk she jumped up and yelled to her colleagues, "This is the book I told you about!" It was clear that she could have kept talking for a lot longer, but after some time I politely cut her off saying I needed to go, because if you're going to be rejected, you might as well handle it efficiently.

Two days later, I was sitting in a diner working away when an email arrived from my agent. At first I was confused and couldn't make out what she was trying to say through all the exclamation marks. It was perplexing to me because my agent doesn't use exclamation marks. She is a straight-up-and-down, spectacle-wearing, native New Yorker who drinks turmeric lattes and appreciates good grammar. She would never waste an exclamation mark for no good reason.

When I got past the overuse of punctuation, there it was in the second glorious paragraph: a book deal. I could have just about kissed the waiter who happened to be refilling my Diet Coke at that very moment.

All up, I have forty-seven rejection emails from the experience, that I might frame one day. Recently my colleague Lucy printed them all out and left them in a pile on my desk. I re-read every single one. At the very bottom she'd printed out the contract for the book deal with a bright Post-it Note: "You only need one yes!"

Success seems easy for some because we're too lazy to look beyond what we first see.

We're led to believe that if we're doing it right, life is easy, and that our sole purpose as humans is to seek more ease and comfort. I believe that's an unhelpful narrative that needs rewriting. We need a different story to tell our children as they lay their heads on their pillows each night. We need to tell the truth and explain that struggle is inevitable, like a next-door neighbor you don't love but have to coexist with. Not only is struggle inevitable, it's also vital. Can we learn how to recognize it yet somehow not let it take over? We need to appreciate the effort, give thanks for the rejection and remember that, at times, one yes is all we need.

play.

I've always believed that life is a game. You give it your best, get good teammates around you, hopefully win more than you lose, but remember that you're going to lose at times anyway, so you might as well have fun doing it.

What we didn't realize before 2020 was just how complacent and safe we were all playing, and how much we were doing things simply because that was the way they had always been done. Yes, we were taking "risks," but on the scale of how much we've all had to change, these risks were small and inconsequential.

I believe we have been thrown a once-in-a-lifetime opportunity to embrace a new model of work and of life, and I want us to catch it with both hands. The nine-to-five day is gone, the office as we know it is gone, and the new model for working requires us to show up with a bunch of fresh skills in order to acclimate and get ahead.

There's a new hustle going on for so many of us right now. Lots of clever people are embracing this new hustle eagerly, with their shoulders back and their eyes wide open. They've discarded the old ways of working and are rebirthing a new version of themselves. On the flipside, there are the types of people who are breathing a sigh of relief that they largely escaped the effects of the pandemic and can now return to life as it was. I understand this thinking—familiar is comfortable, after all—but I also urge us to look a little deeper at the opportunities to come from this extraordinary time.

We now have an opportunity to choose, so let's choose wisely. Let's take the lessons we've learned and turn them into something prevailing and something that matters. We have this chance to build productive teams that stay curious and open, and create inspiring workplaces our people want to come to. We have this beautiful opportunity to question why we do the work that we do and to interrupt old habits that we've now outgrown.

This is your chance to press reset for yourself and the people around you. You can architect a new framework for inspiring your people, helping them see that you're available to them and committed to their new-found freedom and autonomy. You can keep showing up as a radical optimist who encourages positivity everywhere you go, holding space for possibility to thrive among your people and peers.

You can be the one who's switched on to a new way of being, calling forth more creativity, space and freedom, or you can remain stuck in old ways, half asleep and cruising. Now is your chance to reinvent yourself and ultimately run your own race. You have one chance to go start that stock portfolio (just buy one share—start there!) or write the first sentence in that book you've been threatening to write (and then write the second and then the third until it's done), start that business or save the first thousand dollars toward that investment property you want to own in the next few years.

It's time for your breakthrough. Go forth confidently, proudly making the days count. This new hustle is yours. It's yours to design and yours to own. Shoulders back, eyes open— it's time to leap into a different way of being, and it's time to claim *your* new hustle.

Remember this: it's all one big game where you're competing only against yourself to get better. When you play it well, you win. Tag, you're it.

references

RELAX.

Page

19. Parents often appear hurried and overwhelmed...: Emma Isaacs, "The myth of busyness," *Thrive Global*, September 11, 2020, thriveglobal.com/stories/the-myth-of-busyness.

20. For the past five decades, our work hours...: Lydia Saad, "The '40-hour' workweek is actually longer—by seven hours," *Gallup News*, August 14, 2014, news.gallup.com/poll/175286/hour-workweek-actually-longer-seven-hours.aspx.

DETERMINE.

Page

39. A 2017 study by *Harvard Business Review*...: Leslie A. Perlow, Constance Noonan Hadley and Eunice Eun, "Stop the meeting madness," *Harvard Business Review*, July–August 2017, hbr.org/2017/07/stop-the-meeting-madness.

BEND.

Page

82. Despite laws against pregnancy discrimination . . . : Bryan Robinson, PhD, "Pregnancy discrimination in the workplace affects mother and baby health," *Forbes*, July 11 2020, https:// www.forbes.com/sites/bryanrobinson/2020/07/11/pregnancy -discrimination-in-the-workplace-affects-mother-and-baby -health/?sh=417afd92cac6.

ENJOY.

Page

100. According to a Gallup poll, people who . . . : Annamarie Mann, "Why we need best friends at work," *Gallup Workplace*, January 15, 2018, www.gallup.com/workplace/236213/why -need-best-friends-work.aspx.

100. The *Washington Post* recently ran an article . . . : Lisa Bonos, "Admit it. You miss your work spouse.," *Washington Post*, October 12, 2020, www.washingtonpost.com/lifestyle/2020/ 10/12/work-spouse-wife-husband-office.

LEAD.

Page

187. In fact, a Gallup survey revealed that only . . . : Robert Sutton and Ben Wigert, "More harm than good: The truth about performance reviews," *Gallup Workplace*, May 6, 2019, www .gallupcom/workplace/249332/harm-good-truth-performance -reviews.aspx.

OWN.
Page

222. Dick's Sporting Goods said it would no longer . . . : Rachel Siegel, "Dick's Sporting Goods CEO says company will stop selling assault-style rifles, set under-21 ban for other guns," *Washington Post*, March 1, 2018, www.washingtonpost.com/news/business/wp/2018/02/28/dicks-sporting-goods-ceo-says-company-will-no-longer-sell-assault-rifles-guns-to-people-under-21.

special people

As with most hard things worth doing, I didn't attempt this book on my own. Lucy Ormonde showed up again to make *The New Hustle* a project to be proud of, just as she did the first time with *Winging It*. She must enjoy suffering as much as I do, ha! Thanks, Luce, for seeing in me what others often don't and for putting in all the long hours at diners and bars and dodgy airport hotels and our kitchen bench to bring this work alive. We survived, again!

Dani, you're my greatest cheerleader and give me a stupidly imbalanced amount of support. Our friendship is deeply lopsided, and I intend to spend the rest of my life evening it up a little. Morrie, Hayley, Tan—I love that even though oceans separate us, we always pick up where we left off, and I know you'd take my call at 3 a.m. on any day, just as I would yours. Azure, you once told me that the only good thing to come out of 2020 was gaining you as family, and I agree. You've saved me more than once.

To my family—particularly my mama, dad and sister—thanks for being such a calming and sensible force in my life. I most definitely did not inherit a moment of your patience or steadiness, and for the soft landing you give me I'll always be grateful. Poppy—I think I told you enough how lucky I feel to have had you as my grandfather before you stopped being able to hear it.

To Cheryl for being an incredibly understanding editor and for showing immense compassion and kindness always. You're the real deal.

To my Business Chicks team who greet every day with such fierceness and show me what happens when we do the new hustle together. I adore you all.

To our beloved Business Chicks members—thank you for being, and staying, by our sides, particularly during these past few years.

Big huge thanks to Ens and Claire, for keeping the wheels spinning and doing it with such a massive sense of humor. And lastly, to my babies—Milla, Honey, Indie, Ryder, Piper and Louis—for giving me six reasons to keep going.